DIFFICULT WORDS
IN POLISH-ENGLISH TRANSLATION

PWN

DIFFICULT WORDS IN POLISH-ENGLISH TRANSLATION

Wyrazy i wyrażenia trudne do przetłumaczenia na język angielski

Christian Douglas Kozłowska

WYDAWNICTWO NAUKOWE PWN
WARSZAWA 2008

Projekt okładki i stron tytułowych
EDWIN RADZIKOWSKI

Redaktorzy
KAZIMIERZ POLAŃSKI
DOROTA STANISZEWSKA-KOWALAK

Redaktor techniczny
LEONARD ZIELIŃSKI

Korekta
PHILLIP SMITH

ISBN 978-83-01-14288-9

Wydawnictwo Naukowe PWN SA
00-251 Warszawa, ul. Miodowa 10
tel. 022 69 54 321
faks 022 82 67 163
e-mail: pwn@pwn.com.pl
www.pwn.pl

Przedmowa

Przekazujemy Państwu ostatnią już, niestety, pracę uznawanej i szanowanej za swój dorobek, wieloletniej autorki prac z dziedziny leksykologii współpracującej z Wydawnictwem Naukowym PWN. Ten swego rodzaju słowniczek wyrazów najtrudniejszych do przetłumaczenia na język angielski powstawał w trakcie długoletniej praktyki translatorskiej i dydaktycznej autorki. Stanowi on alfabetycznie ułożony zbiór słów wraz z ich angielskimi odpowiednikami. Ich użycie na ogół ilustrują zdania. Po zdaniach w języku polskim następują przykładowe tłumaczenia angielskie. Autorka często wyjaśnia, dlaczego w pewnych przypadkach używamy danych słów lub zwrotów, a nie innych. W wyjaśnieniach tych autorka bierze pod uwagę zagadnienia gramatyczne występujące w obu omawianych językach, użycie idiomów i tak zwane „collocations", czyli wyrazy, z którymi można łączyć dane słowa.

Autorka bardzo umiejętnie wybrała to, co bywa trudne do przełożenia dla mało doświadczonego tłumacza. Wzięła też pod uwagę niuanse językowe i kulturowe. Dlatego też zbiór ten z pewnością posłuży uczącym się języka angielskiego na średnim i zaawansowanym poziomie, jak również tłumaczom polskim tłumaczącym na język angielski.

Zamieszczone słownictwo zostało przez autorkę dobrane bardzo skrupulatnie, niemniej jednak słowniczek ten nie pretenduje do miana pracy wyczerpującej. Mimo to, przekazujemy go Państwu z przekonaniem, że nie zawsze mogąc znaleźć potrzebne Państwu informacje w słownikach dwujęzycznych, będą Państwo mogli z niego właśnie się dużo nauczyć.

REDAKCJA

Administracja

The translation of 'administracja' will depend on what is being administered.

When the thing being administered is a country or larger region, translate 'administracja' as **administration**, meaning a) the body of people who are doing the job of administering, or b) the activity itself of administering, e.g.

1. Szukają formuły, która pozostawiłaby przy władzy brytyjskiego gubernatora i brytyjską administrację.
– They are looking for a formula that would leave a British Governor and **administration** in charge.

2. Jest dziwne, że konserwatywne administracje pozostawiły tę sprawę tak długo nie załatwioną.
– Conservative **administrations** have been curiously supine in leaving the matter for so long.

When the thing being administered (managed) is house property, such as a block of flats, a housing estate, an office block, etc., use the English terms **estate managers / property managers / management office** e.g.

3. Administracja osiedla uprzedziła wszystkich mieszkańców, że nastąpi krótka przerwa w dopływie wody.
– The **estate managers / management office** notified all the tenants that the water would be cut off for a short time.

One can also use the term **managing agents**.

Very often 'administracja' is used, too, in the sense of an action, in which case it should be translated as **administration**, meaning the **activity of** administering, e.g.

4. Odmówił przyjęcia awansu, ponieważ wolał spędzić czas na badaniach naukowych niż na pracy administracyjnej.
– He refused promotion, because he preferred to spend his time on research, rather than **administration**.

Akademik

The Polish word 'akademik' and the English word **academic** are almost identical in appearance, but there is a slight difference of meaning. Here we take these words as referring to people. Some people find it difficult to distinguish between the two.

There is an important difference in meaning between **academic** and **academician**, for an **academician** is someone who is a member/fellow of an illustrious Academy, such as the Académie Française, or the Royal Academy of Arts in Britain (note: of Arts, *not* Art). An **academician** has enormous prestige – much higher than an **academic**.

So to make clear the difference between **academic** and **academician** it may suffice to point out that an **academician** has much higher status and prestige.

Aktualny

Never translate 'aktualny' as **actual. Actual** in English means 'faktyczny', 'rzeczywisty'.

Our choice of English equivalent for 'aktualny' will depend on the noun it accompanies. This will be illustrated by the following examples.

1. To bardzo aktualna uwaga!
– That's a very **apt comment!**

2. Czy nie wiesz przypadkiem, jaka jest aktualna cena złota?
– Do you happen to know the **current price** of gold?

This can also be translated idiomatically:

– Do you happen to know how gold stands **at present?**

3. Czy ten plan zajęć jest nadal aktualny?
– Is this timetable **up-to-date**?

4. Wydawnictwo przekazało nam swój aktualny adres (presumably changed).
– The publishers gave us their **new address**.

5. Czy znasz jego aktualny adres? (not necessarily changed).
– Do you know his **present address?**

6. Praca ta po aktualnych cenach nie opłaca się.
– At the **current rates** that job doesn't pay.

7. Przesyłamy Wam aktualny cennik na części.
– Enclosed please find an **up-to-date** price **list** for spare parts.
– Enclosed please find the **latest** price **list** for spare parts.

8. Czy masz o nich aktualne wiadomości?
– Do you have any **recent news** of them?

9. Kto jest jego aktualną dziewczyną / sympatią?
– Who is his **current girl-friend?**

10. Wojna na Bliskim Wschodzie to jeszcze bardzo aktualny temat w gazetach.
– The war in the Middle East is still **a very topical subject. / / ... very much in the news. /... hitting the headlines**.

11. Aktualna sytuacja na świecie nie jest wesoła.
– The **present-day** world **situation** doesn't look too good.

It will be seen that certain English nouns call for certain adjectives to collocate with them as equivalents of 'aktualny'. We have:

apt: comment, criticism, statement, opinion, remark
current: girl-friend, price, rate, problems, difficulty, worry, task, job, dispute, negotiations, contract, talks
present: address, job, difficulties
present-day: situation
up-to-date: timetable, list, information
latest: girl-friend, list, news
topical: subject

Apart from translating 'aktualny' by a collocating adjective, there are also other, often idiomatic, ways of translating it as well. This may be illustrated by examples where 'aktualny' comes at the end of the sentence, instead of before the noun (as in the sentences above).

Other ways of translating 'aktualny'

12. Czy Wasze zaproszenie jest jeszcze aktualne?
– Do you **still want us** to come?
– Is your invitation **still open**?

13. Czy ta decyzja jest jeszcze aktualna?
– Is that **decision still effective**?
– Does that **decision still hold good**?

14. Czy nasza umowa nadal jest aktualna?
– Does our **agreement still hold good**?
– Is our **agreement still binding**?
– Is our **agreement still valid**?
– Does **what we agreed on still hold**?
– Does our **agreement still stand**?

15. Czy ten plan nadal jest aktualny?
– Does the **plan still hold good**?
– Is the **plan still on**?
– Is it **still the same** plan?

16. Czy dla Ciebie ta sprawa jest nadal aktualna?
– Does that **business still interest** you?
– Do you **still want to go on with** that **business**?

17. Czy zakaz palenia nadal jest aktualny?
– Is the smoking **ban still on**?

18. Czy nasze spotkanie na jutro nadal jest aktualne?
– Is our **meeting** for tomorrow **still on**?
– Do we **still meet** tomorrow **as planned**?

19. To są nasze aktualne problemy.
– These are the problems **we are faced with** at the moment.

20. W referacie zaprezentowano aktualne problemy rozbrojenia.
– The speech dealt with disarmament **problems of today**.

Here too, it will be noticed that certain ways of translating 'aktualny' collocate with certain nouns:

still open: invitation, offer

still binding: decision, rule, regulation, agreement, contract
still hold good: decision, plan, agreement
still on: ban, meeting, plan
still valid: contract, agreement

'Nieaktualne'

21. Spotkanie nie jest już aktualne.
– The meeting **isn't on** any more.
– The meeting **is off**.

22. Dzwonię w sprawie ogłoszenia. (e.g. about a car)
'Już nieaktualne.'
– I'm phoning about the car that's advertised.
– Sorry. It's **already gone**.
– Sorry. It's **already been sold**.

23. Przyszedłem w sprawie posady.
'Już nieaktualne.'
– I've come to enquire about the job.
– Sorry. It's **already been taken**.

24. Regulaminy te są teraz nieaktualne.
– These regulations are now **out of date**.
– These regulations are **no longer in force**.

Badać

In Polish, 'badać' is a verb that can be used in many different situations. It collocates with many nouns. In English, diverse equivalents of it will be used, depending on which noun they *go with*. Generally the noun which is the object of 'badać' determines how 'badać' is translated into English. Some examples are given below. The most appropriate equivalent is given first in sequence, but other collocations are given in alphabetical order, for one access.

badać efekty czegoś – **study, analyse, carry out research on, check, do research on, examine, test** the effects of sth badać hipotezę – **test** a hypothesis

badać nowy lek – **test** a new drug

badać nowy materiał – **test** a new material

badać możliwości – **explore, examine, go into, inquire into, investigate, review, sound out, study**, try to **find out** the possibilities

badać okoliczności – **look into, examine, inquire into, investigate** the circumstances

badać pacjenta – **examine** a patient

badać preparat – **test** a preparation

badać problem – **work on** (esp. a scientific problem), **go into, investigate, study**, **examine** a problem

badać przyczyny czegoś – **examine, go into, investigate, probe**, try to **find out** the causes of (reasons for) **of** sth.

badać przeszłość jakiejś osoby – **investigate**, **look into** sb's past

badać opinię publiczną – **survey, sound out** public opinion

badać reakcje – **test, check, monitor, observe, study** reactions

badać rynek – **survey, sound out, study, carry out** a survey of the market, **do market research**

badać sprawę (affair, case, matter) – **inquire into** an affair, **go into** an affair, **investigate** a case, **look into** a matter, **inquire into** a matter

badać świadka – **examine, question** a witness

badać sytuację – **study, investigate, look into, think about** the situation

badać teorię – **test** a theory

badać teren – (here we should also know the subject of the verb): a geologist will **survey** (= map) the area, the geologist may **explore** the area for mineral resources; during military operations a patrol may be sent out to **reconnoitre** the area

badać właściwości (np. nowego materiału) – **test** the properties of...

badać zbrodnię – **investigate** a crime

badać zjawisko – **study**, **examine** a phenomenon

We may turn these examples round, and give a list of English verbs meaning 'badać', and the nouns which form their object:

carry out / do / research on – a scientific problem, the causes / effects of sth

examine – a patient, the reasons for sth, the circumstances

explore – an area, possibilities

go into – an affair, a matter, the question of sth, the causes of sth, the reasons for sth, a problem (all kinds)

inquire into – an affair, a case, a matter, the circumstances, the possibilities of sth

investigate – the causes of sth, the reasons for sth, a crime, the circumstances of sth, a person's past, the possibilities of sth, a problem (research topic), a situation

observe – sb's reactions to sth

question – a witness

sound out – the market, the possibilities of sth, public opinion, sb's opinion, sb's views on sth

study – a problem (all kinds), the causes of sth, the effects of sth, the market, a phenomenon, the possibilities of sth, sb's reactions, the reasons for sth, a situation

survey – an area, the market, public opinion

test – a new drug, a new material, a new preparation, a hypothesis, a theory, reactions

try to find out – the causes of sth, the reason for sth, the possibilities of sth

work on – a scientific problem

Badania naukowe

In translating 'badania naukowe', several problems arise.

Firstly, should we give the English noun in the singular, or in the plural, i.e. – as often happens – should we translate these two words as **research**, or possibly **researches**? One does not have to feel constrained by the plural form of the Polish noun. There apears to be a subtle difference in usage here, for **research** (singular) seems to have a general connotation, meaning a body of research, whereas **researches** (plural) may be used when referring to separate pieces, or separate series of research.

Here are some examples of such sentences:

Research (singular):

– According to new **research**, penguins can suffer dramatically from the effects of oil pollution, even if their feathers are only lightly contaminated with oil.

– **Research** suggests that fetal exposure to cocaine causes premature birth and low birth weight.

Researches (plural):

– This journal publishes those **researches** that mainstream science has found too difficult to place.

– American **researches** into the causes of cancer have met with some success.

Nevertheless, the singular form (**research**) appears to be much the more common form in English, e.g.

– This study shows that in 1989 Japan started spending a larger percentage of its gross national product on **research** than the US.

Secondly, 'badania naukowe' can also be translated, though less frequently, as **scientific research**. The point is: should the word **scientific** always be included in such translation, or can we omit it? The word scientific appears to be superfluous, because the English word **research** itself already contains the notion of **scientific**, of **study**, etc. **Scientific** is not the exact equivalent of 'naukowe' anyway. So in most cases we use **research** alone, ignoring the word **scientific**. Indeed it is not easy to find an example where both **scientific** and **research** occur together. The following is a rare example:

'The local French authorities placed an embargo on coelacanth specimens from the Comoros, allowing only French scientists to work on them. They even went to the extent of placing injunctions on specimens that they had donated to various museums round the world, allowing them to be used strictly for display purposes only, and very definitely not for **scientific research**. So **research** on the biology and physiology of the coelacanth was severely stifled for many years.' (*New Scientist*, 5th Oct. 1991, p. 49, David Martill reviews "Living Fossil: the Story of the Coelacanth" by Keith S. Thomson, Hutchinson Radius).

Here is another example:

'The organisation English Nature... will fund **scientific research** to establish how many animals (red squirrels and dormice) still survive in isolated woodlands...' (*Observer*, February 1992, in an article by Polly Ghazi: "Heseltine wakes up dormice vote in Tory package for wildlife").

Thirdly, we come to the question of choice of vocabulary. In Polish we find the phrase 'prowadzić badania naukowe nad jakimś problemem', which means: **to investigate / to study** sth, **to do / conduct / carry out / be engaged in research** on sth.

Let us have a look at some right and wrong usages:

WRONG: – A large sum has been put aside for cancer **researches**.
RIGHT: – A large sum has been put aside for cancer **research**.

WRONG: – Professor Smith has been doing **the research** on mutations.
RIGHT: – Professor Smith has been **doing research** on mutations.

WRONG: – He is **leading researches** on the causes of cancer. (literal translation of the Polish 'prowadzić')
RIGHT: – He is **doing research / engaged in research** on the causes of cancer.

Here are some examples of correct language usage taken from advertisements appearing in the *New Scientist*, for job vacancies involving research:

Research Fellowships and Grants

Emeritus Fellowships:

Awards of up to £6,000 a year – to enable persons to complete **a piece of research**.

Post-Doctoral Research Fellowship in the area of **cancer research**.

Fellows will conduct **basic research on...**

You will be expected to **undertake research** preferably in areas of receptor pharmacology...

The post holder will be expected to **undertake** appropriate **research projects** leading to publication.

3. Innovative applicants who can **carry out** their own **research** would be suited to this post.

Let us now see some instances of translations of 'badania naukowe' in which the word **research** is ignored, and replaced by **work** – one of the most useful words in the English language. **Work** is probably the best translation of all for the Polish term 'badania naukowe' in continuous texts.

These sentences, given here in English alone, can be used as models, or patterns, to be followed.

'Badania naukowe' can usefully be translated as **work**:

– This unexpected result is confirmed by the **work** of Smith and Jones.
– Plant virus **work** has lagged behind other studies.
– The **work** of Christian Barnard on heart transplants is well known.
– Brown's **work** on the spread of AIDS has shown that...
– He abandoned his earlier **work** on something, in order to devote himself to something else.
– Hawking is best known for his **work** on black holes.

Baza

'Baza' is a word whose translation will depend on the context, as the following sentences will show.

'Baza' meaning a place where things are collected:

a) Baza autobusowa, tramwajowa, itd.

1. Po godzinie jedenastej autobusy wracają do bazy.
– After eleven, the buses go back to their **depots**.

b) Baza okrętów wojennych

2. Aby dostać się do bazy marynarki wojennej, trzeba mieć przepustkę.
– You have to have a pass to be able to get into a **naval base**.

c) Baza dla samolotów wojskowych

3. Trzy samoloty myśliwskie nie wróciły do bazy.
– Three fighters failed to return to **base**.

4. Wszystkie bazy lotnicze w Wielkiej Brytanii zostały postawione w stan gotowości.
– All the **RAF bases** were put on alert.

'Baza' meaning a starting point:

5. Alpiniści założyli bazę na wysokości 3 tys. m.
– The climbers set up their **base camp** at an altitude of 3,000 metres.

'Baza' in a figurative sense:

6. Musimy rozwijać krajową bazę surowcową.
– We must develop our own **supplies / resources** of raw materials.

So, depending on the context, possible translations of 'baza' are: **depot, (naval) base, base, base camp, supplies, resources**.

'Baza' also means the bottom part of an object, e.g.

7. W Londynie gołębie strasznie brudzą bazę pomnika Nelsona.
– In London the pigeons make an awful mess of the **base** of Nelson's Column.

Budownictwo

The Polish word 'budownictwo' has several different meanings, as may be deduced from the following examples. It may mean **the building industry** or **the building trade**:

Dzisiejsze czasy są trudne dla budownictwa:
– The **building industry / building trade** is going through hard times at present.

Szukam mieszkania do wynajęcia w starym budownictwie.
– Wanted – Flat to let in **pre-war building** (indicating **type** of building wanted).

Nasza firma otrzymała 2000 m kw. z przeznaczeniem na budownictwo mieszkaniowe.
– Our firm has acquired 2,000 sq m of land for **housing development**.

Some terms are based on the type of building proposed, e.g.

budownictwo przemysłowe – **industrial building** or **industrial construction,**
budownictwo mostów – **bridge building**.

Other terms are connected with the buildings' appearance, type of architecture, type of construction, e.g.

niskie budownictwo – **low-rise buildings**.
budownictwo wysokie – **high-rise buildings**,
budownictwo monumentalne – **monumental buildings**.

Note that the meaning of **building** in English depends in part on the presence or absence of the definite article, i.e. when preceded by *the* or *a*, **building** usually means 'gmach'; **building** not preceded by any article is a verbal noun, indicating the **activity of building**, e.g.

Building is very tiring work.
The building we are erecting is going to be a very tall one.

Budzić

The simple meaning of 'budzić' is 'to **waken** sb from sleep'. But it can be used metaphoricaly in a wide variety of contexts and senses expressing emotion.

In such cases, the English translation of 'budzić' varies with the verb's direct object. When translating such sentences, begin first by choosing an English equivalent for the noun that is the verb's object. Then decide which English verb would collocate with that English noun.

Some examples are given below:

budzić antagonizm – **arouse, cause, create, lead to, excite** antagonism
budzić entuzjazm – **arouse, cause, create, generate, give rise to, stir up** enthusiasm
budzić kontrowersję – **arouse, cause, create, excite, generate, give rise to, stir up** controversy
budzić miłość – **awaken, kindle** love for sb

budzić nadzieję – **kindle, (re)awaken** hope

budzić nienawiść wśród ludzi – **sow** hatred among people

budzić niechęć do kogoś – **arouse, create, foment, stir up** ill will towards sb., **make sb.** dislike sb. else

budzić niezadowolenie – **give rise to** discontent, **give rise to** dissatisfaction

budzić opór (w stosunku do kogoś /czegoś) – **stir up** opposition, resistance to a plan, an idea, etc.

budzić oburzenie – **arouse, cause, give rise** to indignation

budzić podejrzenie – **arouse** suspicion

budzić podziw – **arouse** admiration

budzić ponure myśli – **lead** to gloomy thoughts

budzić pragnienie czegoś – **awaken** a desire for sth

budzić pozytywną reakcję – **elicit, obtain, produce** a positive / favourable / satisfactory reaction

budzić szacunek do kogoś – **awaken** respect for sb, **make** sb respect sb

budzić urazę – **cause, stir up** resentment

Bywa i tak, że ...

This phrase can be translated in a number of different ways:

a) by using as the principal clause the phrases **It sometimes happens..., It occasionally happens..., It happens from time to time...**, followed by a subordinate clause beginning with **that...**

b) by using the adverbs **occasionally, sometimes** (with no subordinate **that** clause). These adverbs are best placed at the beginning of the sentence.

c) by using the phrases **There are times when..., There are instances of...** (*watch the construction*).

The above variants appear to be interchangeable, e.g.

Bywa i tak, że samolot nie może odlecieć z powodu złej pogody.
– **It sometimes happens** that a plane can't take off because of bad weather.
– **It occasionally happens** that a plane can't take off because of bad weather.

– **From time to time it happens** that a plane can't take off because of bad weather.
– **Occasionally** a plane can't take off because of bad weather.
– **Sometimes** a plane can't take off because of bad weather.
– **There are times when** a plane can't take off because of bad weather.
– **There are instances** of a plane being unable to take off because of bad weather (*note the construction*).

Cały

When translating the Polish word 'cały', a number of patterns are available to us. These patterns may contain the English words **all**, or **entire**, or **whole** as an adjective, or **whole** as a noun, or **throughout**, or **throughout the whole of sth**.

Here are some examples using **all**.

When 'cały' qualifies a Polish collective noun which is translated into English as an ordinary plural noun, such as *personel, młodzież*, etc. then 'cały' is translated as **all**, and the verb is given in the plural form, e.g.

– cały personel tej fabryki
– **all the workers** at the factory
– cała młodzież akademicka
– **all the students**

All is also used in certain stock phrases, e.g.

Cała ludzkość – **all** mankind

All can be used with *day, week, month, year*. One can also use the word **whole**, e.g.

– I did nothing **all** day yesterday, or:
– I did nothing the **whole** day yesterday.
– I have been ill **all** month, or:
– I have been ill the **whole** month.
– I shall be busy **all** next year, or:

– I shall be busy **during the whole of** next year.
– I slept **all day** on Tuesday, or:
– I slept **the whole day** on Tuesday.

All is also used in the following kinds of construction:

– Tom ate **all** the pudding.
– No one **in all the world** is as wonderful as you.
– **all the beauty** in the world
– Have you eaten **all the ice-cream?**

Coming back to the use of the word **whole**, here are several examples in which it occurs:

produkcja całego przemysłu
– the output of industry **as a whole** (this can also be translated as **total** industrial output)

Dialogue:

Ann: Have you read **the whole** book?
Tom: Yes, I've read **the whole** of it.

Now take the case of two adjectives qualifying one noun. One would never say 'throughout his **whole** long life', or 'you must eat the **whole** big apple.' In both cases the noun is already qualified so we say 'throughout the **whole of** his long life', and 'eat the **whole of** this big apple'. In these two cases, **whole** is used us a noun.

Speaking of mankind, we say 'the **whole of** mankind', never 'the **whole** mankind'. One never says 'the mankind', therefore one cannot say 'the **whole** mankind.' Again, 'mankind' is a special kind of uncountable noun, and is always used without the article.

The word **entire** can usually be used instead of **whole**. It is used as an adjective, but not always. For example, it would be rather strange to say 'the **entire** apple', for **entire** belongs to somewhat more formal style.

Words that collocate with **entire**:

– He spent his **entire** income on drink.
– He spent his **whole** life collecting butterflies.

Cechować

Sometimes, in translation, we can leave out the word 'cechować' altogether, e.g.

1. Cechowała go duża kultura osobista.
– (One could see that) he was a very civilised man. / he had excellent manners. / he was a real gentleman.

2. Cechowała go niezwykła pracowitość.
– He was exceptionally hardworking.
– His assiduity was remarkable.

Or we can use some equivalent of 'cechować', e.g.

3. Po wojnie kraje Dalekiego Wschodu cechowała duża dynamika ekonomiczna.
– After the war, rapid economic growth **was characteristic of** the countries of the Far East.
– After the war, **a distinctive feature of** the Far Eastern countries was rapid economic growth.

4. Mówił cicho, bez energii, bez tej pasji, które zwykle cechowały każdy jego występ.
– He spoke in a low voice, without the energy and passion that **generally characterised** (**accompanied**) his every speech.

5. Cechowała go niezwykła wytrwałość.
– One of his **attributes** was exceptional tenacity.
– One of his **character traits** was tremendous perseverance.
– **He was noted for** his tremendous perseverance.

6. Połączenie wysokiego przyrostu naturalnego z niską produkcją ekonomiczną jest typową cechą krajów dopiero rozwijających się.
– A high birth-rate accompanied by low economic growth is **characteristic of** developing countries.

Cel

'Cel' is a word that has many equivalents in English, e.g. **aim, goal, purpose, target, end, end-purpose, destination, mark, object, objective**, so that the choice of language is very wide.

When in turn we match each of these with various possible collocations, we can have a real tapestry of language.

Among the most concrete, down-to-earth translations of 'cel' (as in 'cel podróży') is **destination**, e.g.

> Po ośmiu godzinach jazdy nareszcie dobijaliśmy do celu naszej podróży.
> – After about eight hours' travelling we at last reached our **destination**.

> Poruszając się w nieznanym terenie, najlepiej jest dążyć do jakiegoś widocznego celu, np. do wieży kościelnej.
> – When moving through unknown territory, the best thing to do is to make for some distinctive **landmark**, such as a church spire.

Goal can be used in a figurative sense, too, as in:

> – try to **achieve** a **goal**, **reach** a **goal**.

'Cel' can also mean **target**, both in the most concrete, literal sense and in the meaning of some achievement, or desired goal, e.g.

> Na wczorajszych zawodach strzeleckich nasz syn miał niesamowite szczęście, bo trafił w sam środek celu (w sam środek tarczy),
> – In yesterday's shooting match our son had tremendous luck, for he scored a **bull's eye**,
> ... ale kiedy indziej chybiał celu.
> – ... but on another occasion he was off **target** / missed **the mark**.

But 'cel' is frequently used in a more abstract sense, e.g.

> cel czyjejś miłości – the **object** of someone's affections (love).
> cel czyjejś nienawiści – the **object** of someone's hatred.

'Cel' is frequently translated as **aim**, e.g.

Głównym celem życia Dawida było zrobić fortunę.
– David's main **aim** in life was to make a lot of money.

But we can also say:

– Making money was the **end purpose** of his life.

or:

Co miał na celu?
– What was his **object**?
– What **was** he **after**?

Again, we may hear:

Zyski z wczorajszego balu przeznaczono na cele dobroczynne.
– The money raised from yesterday's ball is **to go to** charity.

Note the following collocations:

– to **achieve** a **goal** – to **win** the **object** of one's affections – to **attain** a **goal** – to **reach** a **goal** – to **achieve** one's **purpose**.

osiągnąć cel – to achieve **one's aim**
wałęsać się bez celu – to wander around **aimlessly**
cel uświęca środki – the **end** justifies the means
życiowy cel – **aim in** life

Co on miał na celu?
– What was he **aiming at**? / What was his **object**? / What **was** he **after**?

Charakter

We must distinguish between the different meanings of 'charakter', for that will affect our choice of translation.

I. When 'charakter' denotes a collection of psychological or moral traits, 'mieć ... charakter' will be rendered as: **have a ... character**. Note the use of the verb **have**:

1. Jej mąż ma trudny charakter.
– Her husband **has** a difficult **character**.

II. When 'charakter' (without an adjective) means *a strong character*, we can translate as follows:

2. On ma charakter, da sobie radę w życiu!
– He'**s got character**, he'll get on all right in life! (= determination, resilience, will to work, etc.)

3. On ma charakter. Wszyscy go szanują za jego zasady.
– He'**s** a man **of character**. Everyone respects him for his principles (honesty, high-mindedness, etc.).

III. If 'charakter' means *type*, the English translation of 'mieć ... charakter' will use, not the verb **to have**, but the verb **to be**, and with one of the following two prepositional constructions:

a) **be ... in character**:

4. Jego wystąpienie miało charakter polityczny.
– His speech **was** political **in character**.

b) **be of a ... character**:

5. W późniejszych latach jego muzyka miała inny charakter.
– In later years, his compositions **were of a** different **character**.

Note that the phrase 'mieć inny charakter' (meaning *type*) can be translated in three different ways:

6. Jego ostatnia symfonia ma charakter inny niż poprzednie
– His last symphony **is different in character to / is of a different character to / differs in character from** the others.

IV. Sometimes to denote either *psychological and moral traits* or *type*, we can use the word **nature** instead of **character**, e.g.

a) *psychological or moral traits*:

7. Józefina miała bardzo łagodny charakter.
– Josephine **had** a very gentle **nature**.

b) *type:*

8. Nie należy tak przejmować się czymś, co ma charakter tymczasowy.
– You shouldn't worry so much about things **of** a passing **nature**.

V. Sometimes we can translate 'charakter' as **form**:

9. Zebranie ma mieć jaki charakter? Formalny czy nieformalny?
– What **form** is the meeting to take? Formal or informal?

This occurs especially when 'charakter' is followed by another noun in the genetive case (*dopełniacz*). Note the constructions: **be in the form of..., take the form of ..., take a ... form**.

10. Jego nowy utwór ma charakter fugi.
– His new piece **is in the form of** a fugue.

11. Powstanie miało charakter buntu chłopskiego.
– The uprising **took the form of** a peasant rebellion.

VI. The phrase 'w charakterze czegoś' can be translated simply by the word **as**:

12. Bywał często u nas w charakterze gościa.
– He often stayed with us **as** a guest.

Note. To denote type or form, never say: **have the character of ...**

VII. Sometimes the English word **character** is closer in meaning to 'atmosfera' or 'indywidualność' in Polish, e.g.

– With its cobbled streets and picturesque old houses, Rye is still a little town with a lot of **character**.

Only some meanings of 'charakter' are discussed here. There remains the question of how to choose between the above equivalents. They overlap in meaning, but are not exact synonyms, so are not always interchangeable. Difference of meaning here is not an isolated question. It is also bound up with type of verb construction, and above all with collocations (particularly noun-noun, but also adjective-noun). These three elements – meaning, verb construction, and collocations – are mutually dependent.

*

The dividing line between **character** and **nature** is a very fine one. In some cases we may not be sure whether to use **character** or **nature**, but the diagram given below may be of some help. Some English collocations are given.

ADJECTIVES WITH PEOPLE	
Character	**Nature**
determined, difficult, dominating, mean, nasty, stable, unstable, stubborn	attractive, cruel, cheerful, domineering, easygoing, energetic, generous, gentle, kind, lively, retiring, sensitive, shy, sweet

It will be seen that **character** attracts collocates connected with moral judgements, whereas **nature** connects with words expressing personality and degree of attractiveness to others.

We say:

John has a very difficult **character**. He's always quarrelling.
Mary has a sweet **nature**. Everyone likes her.
Jim has a strong **character**. He's very determined.
Tom, on the other hand, has a weak **character**, he's easily tempted.

The next diagram may help us to distinguish between the position of the different adjectives in this group, and in particular to distinguish between **character** and **nature**.

Note when to use **has**, and when to use **is of**. Some examples are given below.

PEOPLE	
Psychological traits	
Sb has a ... **character** difficult mean outgoing (un)stable strong stubborn	Sb has a ... **nature** friendly gentle generous happy happy-go-lucky impulsive kindly pleasant sensitive simple straightforward
THINGS	
of a ... kind	
frightening outstanding strange unique unusual	disgusting mysterious pleasant pleasurable secret strange unexpected

Charakterystyczny

A. 'Charakterystyczny' meaning **usual**: translate as **characteristic, typical, usual**, e.g.

1. Bogate zdobnictwo jest charakterystyczną cechą baroku.
– Rich ornamentation is a **characteristic** feature of the baroque (usually found in that style).

2. Nadmierna pobudliwość jest charakterystycznym przejawem takiej osobowości.
– Hyperactivity is a **distinctive feature** of this kind of personality (usually found in that kind of personality).

3. Rozpoczął pracę z charakterystycznym dla siebie entuzjazmem.
– He embarked on this work with his **customary** enthusiasm (generally observable in him).

4. Takie zachowanie jest dla niego charakterystyczne.
– That kind of behaviour is **typical** of him.

(Note the preposition **of** in the above sentences).

B. 'Charakterystyczny' meaning **specific** to someone or something, different from others: translate as **distinctive**, e.g.

5. Każdy gatunek zwierząt ma szereg charakterystycznych cech, które odróżniają go od innych gatunków.
– Every species of animal has a series of **distinctive** traits which mark it off from other species (e.g. the giraffe's long neck, the zebra's black and white stripes, etc.).

6. Przy jego charakterystycznym głosie łatwo można było rozpoznać, kto mówi.
– With his **distinctive** voice it was very easy to recognise who was speaking.

To illustrate the difference between parts **A** and **B**, compare the following:

7. Książka ta jest bardzo charakterystyczna dla twórczości tego autora.
– The book is very **characteristic of** the author's work (similar to his other books).

8. Pisarz ten ma swój charakterystyczny styl, który odróżnia go od innych pisarzy tej epoki.
– The writer has a **distinctive** style of his own, which marks him off from other writers of the period.

Charakteryzować

This word has two meanings – or even three if we count the reflexive form. 'Charakteryzować' sb or sth sometimes means **to describe**, e.g.

1. Autor charakteryzuje te tereny z punktu widzenia ekonomicznego i geograficznego.
– The author **describes** these territories from an economic and geographical point of view.

but it can also mean **to distinguish**, e.g.

2. Krajobraz północnej Afryki charakteryzują palmy.
– Palm trees are **distinctive feature** of the landscape of North Africa.

3. Ludzie tego plemienia charakteryzuje wielkie zamiłowanie do walki.
– The people of this tribe are **marked by** their love of fighting.

Reflexive form:

4. Wczesne średniowiecze charakteryzowało się ignorancją i okrucieństwem.
– The early Dark Ages **were marked** by ignorance and cruelty.

Or, one can turn the English sentence round:

– Ignorance and cruelty were **typical** (**characteristic**) features of life in the Dark Ages.

Dopiero

In most cases, the meaning of 'dopiero' is connected with time. But occasionally, instead of time it denotes emphasis. There are other, idiomatic meanings as well.

An outline of the plan we propose to follow is given below.

I. TIME

A. *The simplest ways of translating 'dopiero' (relating to time), when we have in the Polish text:*

1) 'Dopiero' + Verb

2) 'Dopiero' + Adverb, Adverbial Phrase, Adverbial Clause (Past, Present, Future)

3) 'Dopiero' + Present Participle

B. *Other ways of translating 'dopiero' referring to time.*

II. POSITION IN A SEQUENCE

III. EMPHASIS

Affirmative and negative statements, sentences 29–31.

IV. IDIOMATIC EXAMPLES

Sentences 32, 33

V. EXTRA PRACTICE

A. Time: Sentences 1–5
B. Not time: Sentence 6

*

I. TIME

A. *Simple ways of translating 'dopiero' referring to time:*

1) 'Dopiero' + Verb **– just, only just**

1. Pociąg dopiero co odszedł.
– The train has **just** left.
– The train has **only just** left.

Moment of speaking		Polish tense	English tense
Past	Present	Past	Perfect
just **only just**			

Note that **just** denotes closeness to the time of speaking. Nearness to the time of speaking is even more marked if we add **only** before **just**, as in the second of the above sentences.

2. Dopiero jadłeś, a już jesteś głodny!
– You've **just** eaten, and you're hungry **already**!

Note the word order. **Already hungry** would express a fact, neutral in mood, referring to time only, whereas **hungry already** denotes not only time, but also surprise.

3. Kiedy nareszcie przyjechałem na dworzec, pociąg dopiero co odszedł.
– When I finally **arrived** at the station, the train had **just** left.

Note the tenses: simple past in the subordinate clause, past perfect in the principal clause (comp. with sentence 1).

2) 'Dopiero' + Adverb, Adverbial Phrase, Adverbial Clause

Past

'Dopiero niedawno': **only recently**

4. Dopiero niedawno zastosowano nową metodę w tej fabryce.
– The new method has **only recently** come into use in this factory.

Note that **only recently** is not so close to the moment of speaking as **just** or **only just**.

Moment of speaking			Polish tense	English tense
Past		Present	Past	Perfect
just	**only just**	**only recently**		(action still going on)

– It is **not very long since** the new method was introduced in this factory.
– In this factory the new method **has not** been in use **very long**.

'Dopiero wczoraj' **only yesterday, just ... yesterday, not until yesterday**

5. Dopiero wczoraj: dowiedziałem się, że zmarł jego ojciec.
– I **only** learned **yesterday** that his father had died.

Note: It would be more correct to put **only** immediately before **yesterday**, as that is the word it qualifies, but the colloquial word order given above is more common. The same applies to **just**.

– I **just** learned **yesterday** that his father had died.

Other possible translations:

– I didn't learn **until yesterday** that his father had died.
– It was **only yesterday** that I learned his father had died.

Note the negated verb, which emphasizes more strongly the lateness of learning about the death. It stresses the emptiness of the gap before such and such a thing happened.

Note the English tense here after 'dopiero' is the simple past, because the action of learning is complete.

'Dopiero po...': **It was only after ... that ...**

6. Dopiero po jakimś czasie zdał sobie sprawę, że ją kochał.
– **It was only after** some time **that** he realised he loved her.

7. Dopiero po kilku dniach dowiedziałem się, że wyjechał.
– **It was only after** a few days (some days later) **that** I learned he had left.

8. Nasz kraj dopiero po wojnie rozwinął przemysł na tak dużą skalę.
– **It was not until after** the war **that** Poland developed industry on such a large scale.

'Dopiero w...':

only (*affirmative construction*)
not ... till (*negative construction*)
It was not till (*negative construction*)

9. Stefan dopiero w zeszłym roku zdał maturę.

Affirmative construction (best):

– Stephen **only** got his School Certificate last year.

Note: It would be more correct to place **only** before **last year**, but the more common colloquial word order is given here.

Negative construction:

– Stephen did**n't** get his School Certificate **till** last year.
– It wasn'**t till** last year **that** Stephen got his School Certificate.

Note: When a negative construction is used, there is more emphasis on the period being longer than desired. The construction **it was not till**, or **it was not until** is the most emphatic of all.

10. Dopiero w obecnym stuleciu kobiety uzyskały większe równouprawnienie.
– **It was not until** this century **that** women achieved greater equality.

'Dopiero wtedy, kiedy ...': **only after**

11. Poznałem go dopiero wtedy, kiedy mnie minął.
– It was **only after** he had passed that I recognised him.

Note the pluperfect tense of **passed**.

Present

'Dopiero teraz': **only ... now, only now**

12. Dopiero teraz zdaję sobie sprawę, że muszę polegać na samym sobie.
– **Only now** do I realise that I can only depend on myself.

Note that when **only now** comes at the beginning of the sentence, we must reverse the order of the subject and the verb. Instead of **I realise**, we must put **do I realise**.

13. Tyle czasu minęło, a ty mówisz mi o tym dopiero teraz!
– All that time has passed, and you **only** tell me about it **now!**

14. Ona chorowała poważnie przez kilka miesięcy i dopiero teraz dochodzi do siebie.
– She has been seriously ill for several months, and is **only** getting over it **now**.

Note that sometimes **only** and **now** are juxtaposed, and sometimes they are separated.

'Dopiero po ...': **only afterwards**

15. Lubimy zaczynać wolno, a dopiero po jakimś czasie rozkręcamy się.
– We like to begin slowly, and **only** get going **afterwards**.

'Dopiero jutro...': **not until tomorrow**

16. Dopiero jutro będę wiedziała, czy będę mogła iść do teatru, czy nie.
– I wo**n't** know **until** tomorrow if I'll be able to go to the theatre or not.

Note the negative construction in English.

'Dopiero wtedy, kiedy ...': **not until**

17. Pojedziemy dopiero wtedy, kiedy Anna odrobi lekcje.
– We wo**n't** leave **until** Anna has done her homework.

Note the negative construction in English.

It seems that the future form of 'dopiero' should be translated by a negative verb in the future tense, followed by **until**.

But the following affirmative construction, along with **but only when** is also possible in some cases:

18. Pojadę, ale dopiero wtedy, jak będę miał więcej czasu.
– I'll go, **but only when** I have more time.

3) 'Dopiero' + Present Participle

19. kraje podejmujące dopiero dzieło industrializacji ...
– countries **only beginning to** switch over to industrialisation ...
– countries **only now switching over to** industrialisation ...

B. *Other ways of translating 'dopiero' referring to time:*

First

20. Motyw ten pojawia się w malarstwie dopiero w XV w. n.e.
– This motif **first** appears in painting in the 15th century.

Only later

21. Czy styl ten pojawił się w średniowieczu, czy dopiero w renesansie?
– Did that style first appear in the Middle Ages, or **only later**, in the Renaissance?

Note: Compare with sentence 20.

It took + measure adverbial + before ...

22. Odzyskał dobre imię dopiero w dwa lata potem.
– **It was two years before** he regained his good name.
– **It took him two years before** he regained his good name.
– **It took him two years to** regain his good name.

Only, alone

23. Czas dopiero pokaże, co z tego wyniknie.
– **Only** time will show what will come of it.
– Time **alone** will show what will come of it.

Note that **only** comes before the noun, whereas **alone** comes after it.

Only

24. To wczesna godzina jeszcze! To dopiero siódma!
– It's early yet – it's **only** seven o'clock!

25. Mój syn ma dopiero dwa lata.
– My son is **only** two.

II. POSITION IN A SEQUENCE

Sometimes 'dopiero' indicates position in a sequence, as can be seen in the following examples:

26. Dopiero trzeci strzał go trafił.
– It was the **third** shot that **finally** got him.

27. Ciągle rodziła synów, a dopiero piąte dziecko okazało się córeczką.
– She kept giving birth to boys, and **only** the fifth baby turned out to be a girl.

28. Napisał wcześniej trzy sztuki teatralne, ale dopiero czwarta odniosła prawdziwy sukces.
– He had written three plays already, but it was **only** the fourth one that was a real success.

III. EMPHASIS

Here 'dopiero' has no connection with time. 'Cóż dopiero' here rather has the meaning of 'tym bardziej'.

Affirmative statement:

29. Łatwo przekonał prawnika, a cóż dopiero mnie, laika!
– He was able to convince the lawyer easily, **to say nothing of me**, a layman.
– He was able to convince the lawyer, **so it was easy enough** to convince a layman like me!

Negative statements:

30. Nie mógł nawet przekonać mnie, a cóż dopiero prawnika!
– He couldn't even convince me, **let alone** the lawyer!
– He couldn't even convince me, **far less** the lawyer!
– He couldn't even convince me, **not to mention** the lawyer!

31. Tego nikt nie śmiałby pomyśleć, a cóż dopiero napisać!
– No one would have dared to think it, **far less** write it!

Note: We cannot use the phrase **not to mention ...** here, as it does not fit in with the infinitive form of the verb.

IV. IDIOMATIC EXAMPLES

The examples given below are unconnected with time.

32. To dopiero pech!
– What bad luck!
– That's rotten luck!
– That's done it!
– That's torn it!

33. A to dopiero złośnik!
– What a temper!
– Did you ever see such grumpy little boy?
– What a bad tempered little beast!

V. EXTRA PRACTICE:

A. *Time*

1. Dopiero teraz przyszłam.
– I've **only just** come.
– I **only** came **a moment ago**.

2. Może ostatnie głosowanie odbędzie się dopiero w przyszłym tygodniu.
– Maybe the final vote **won't** take place **till** next week.

3. Na wyspie Thera, dopiero w późnym okresie minojskim pojawiają się wyraźne ślady kultu.
– On the island of Thera, distinct traces of religious practices **first** begin to appear in the Late Minoan period.

4. Prawdopodobnie sanktuaria domowe i nisze w fortyfikacjach pojawiają się dopiero z końcem epoki mykeńskiej.
– Probably the domestic sanctuaries and the niches in the fortifications **first** appeared towards the end of the Mycenaean period.

5. Samochód zniknął za zakrętem, a dopiero wtedy zrozumiała, że go kocha.
– The car disappeared round the bend, and **it was only then that** she realised she loved him.

(Note the construction: **It was only then that ...**)

B. *Not time*

6. Ja jestem ciągle zajęta, mimo że mam tylko jedno dziecko – a cóż dopiero ona, która ma siedmioro!
– I'm kept busy all the time, and I have only one child – **so what must she be like** with seven!

7. Czy to rzeczywiście ty, Andrzej?
Tak, to ja.
A to dopiero niespodzianka!
– Is that really you, Andrew?
– Yes, it's me.
– Gosh, **what a surprise!** / Well, **this is a surprise**!

Dotychczas

'Dotychczas' is an adverb which can best be translated by a phrase such as: **so far, to date, till now, up till now, till then**, etc.
Some examples are given below:

1. Nic z tego, co dotychczas robił nie wskazywało, że kiedyś będzie tak wybitny.
– Nothing he had done **so far** ever suggested that some day he would be so eminent.

2. Z przebiegu rozmów nic dotychczas nie wskazywało na możliwość zbliżenia poglądów.
– Nothing **hitherto** in the talks had given any indication that agreement might be reached.

3. Dotychczas wszystkie nasze wysiłki były daremne.
– **Up till now**, all our efforts have been in vain.

4. Dotychczas wyniki nie są dobre.
– The results **to date** have not been good.
– **Thus far / So far**, the results have not been good.

Dotychczasowy

Note the following sentences:

1. Dotychczasowa dzialalność dyrektora zasługuje na pochwałę.
– The manager should be congratulated on his work **to date**.
– The manager's track **record** is worthy of praise.

2. Dotychczasowy system rekrutacji na wyższe uczelnie pozostawiał z pewnością wiele do życzenia.
– The **previous** system of university selection undoubtedly left much to be desired.

3. Mamy dokonać oceny dotychczasowego postępu.
– Our job is to assess what progress has been made **so far**.

4. Dotychczasowe wyniki nie są zadowalające.
– Results **up till now** have not been satisfactory.

5. dotychczasowy prezydent
– the **retiring** chairman

6. dotychczasowy rząd
– the **outgoing** government

7. Na podstawie dotychczasowych wyników możemy być nastawieni optymistycznie.
– On the basis of **results so far** we have every right to be optimistic.

8. Z dotychczasowych obserwacji wynika, że...
– **Observation has shown** that...

Note 1. No special English word for 'dotychczasowy' is needed here, as the meaning of 'dotychczasowy' is conveyed by the tense of the verb.

Note 2. Whereas in Polish 'obserwacja' is used in the plural, in English we use the singular noun – **observation**.

Działać

Note the following sentences:

1. W tej sprawie ojciec działał bez mojej wiedzy.
– In that matter, my father **acted** without my knowledge.

2. Jeśli ktoś chce cokolwiek osiągnąć, musi działać energicznie.
– If you want to get on, you have to **pursue your aims** energetically.

3. Jerzy działał w dobrej wierze.
– George **acted** in good faith.

4. Nie wiadomo, czy ta metoda będzie działać, czy nie, ale zaraz zobaczymy.
– We don't know if this method will **work** or not, but we'll soon see.

5. Lekarstwo, które lekarz ostatnio mi zapisał, rzeczywiście działa rewelacyjnie.
– The medicine the doctor gave me recently really has **worked** like magic.

6. Pralka przestała działać, więc muszę wezwać kogoś, aby ją naprawił.
– The washing machine **isn't working**, so I'll have to call somebody in to put it right.

7. Te stare metody nie działają.
– These old methods don't **work**.

Note sentences 1, 2, 3, where 'działać' means **act** or **do something**, and sentences 4, 5, 6, 7, where 'działać' means **work successfully**.

Działalność

Note these sentences:

1. Elżbieta zajmuje się działalnością charytatywną na rzecz niewidomych.
– Elizabeth does **charity work** for the blind.

2. Edward jest ciągle zajęty działalnością polityczną.
– Edward is constantly busy with his **political activities**.

3. Ewa zajmuje się działalnością charytatywną na rzecz bezdomnych.
– Eve does **voluntary work** to help the homeless.

The above sentences describe unpaid work done by volunteers to help the less fortunate. But here is a sentence describing the functioning of some commercial or other organisation:

4. W sobotę o godz. 16 inauguruje swoją działalność pierwsza polska prywatna telewizja satelitarna.
– At 4 o'clock on Saturday afternoon 'Polsat', Poland's first private satellite TV station will **begin broadcasting**.

In sentences 1, 2 and 3, the 'działalność' is morally motivated by a desire to do good. So in translation we have: **charity work, political activities** and **voluntary work**.

In sentence 4, however, there is no mention of an uplifting motive. In fact, there is no direct reference to any motivation behind the activities taking place. So the words **activity** or **work** are not even mentioned.

Dziedzina (w dziedzinie czegoś)

We may take the following as English equivalents of the Polish word 'dziedzina': **branch** (of science, learning), **domain** (of literature, philosophy, etc.), **field** (of knowledge), **line** (of business), **range, scope** (of activity), **sphere** (of learning, culture), **walk** (of life).

In the examples given above, the kind of 'dziedzina' is not specified.

Now we can qualify the situation, where 'dziedzina' is modified in the simplest way, by adding *this* / *that* or *all*, e.g.

> postępy w dziedzinie – progress in this field / in this area,
> we wszystkich dziedzinach nauki – in all spheres of learning
> zainteresowanie w tej dziedzinie – interest in that sort of thing (*colloq*),
> XYZ jest znany w dziedzinie sztuki – XYZ is well-known in the art world.

Sometimes the English equivalent for 'dziedzina' is given, while in other cases it is omitted.

The Poles say: w dziedzinie sportu, w dziedzinie sztuk pięknych, w dziedzinie medycyny.

The English say: in sport, in art, in medicine, e.g.

> Trzeba podjąć ważne decyzje w dziedzinie kopalnictwa węgla kamiennego w Polsce.
> – Important decisions will have to be taken with regard to the coal mining industry in Poland.

Professor S jest najwybitniejszym specjalistą w Polsce w dziedzinie kardiologii.
– Professor S is Poland's most eminent cardiology specialist.
– Professor S is the most eminent cardiologist in Poland.

In other words, it is preferable to omit the English word for 'dziedzina'. The two languages differ here. Polish is fond of constructions consisting of one noun followed by another noun in the genetive case (dopełniacz). But sometimes exceptions occur, e.g.

Piotr ma dużo wiadomości z dziedziny komputerów.
– Best version: Peter knows a lot about computers (*colloq*).
We can say: **in the field of**, but this is not really a typical English construction.

In other words, in Polish texts sometimes we use the phrase 'w dziedzinie czegoś', while in other cases omitting it in the English translation, e.g.

Był to okres pozytywnych przemian w dziedzinie oświaty.
– This was a period of propitious change in education.

The golden rule would seem to be: to keep the text as simple as possible. Here are some sequences:

1. Pomimo licznych interwencji nic się nie zmieniło w tej dziedzinie.
– Although a number of people have tried to intervene, nothing has changed.

2. Robimy znaczne postępy w tej dziedzinie.
– We are making considerable progress is this field.

3. Wiele się ostatnio zmieniło w dziedzinie współpracy międzynarodowej.
– A lot of things have changed recently in the **sphere** of international co-operation.

4. Profesor Smith jest mistrzem w swojej dziedzinie.
– Professor Smith is outstanding in his **special field**.

5. Sam się dziwię, bo nigdy nie podejrzewałem siebie o zainteresowanie się tą dziedziną.
– I'm surprised myself, for I never suspected I would be interested in **that sort of thing** (*colloq*).

6. Komputery odgrywają coraz większą rolę we wszystkich dziedzinach nauki.
– Computers are increasingly important in **all branches of research**.

7. Występują jeszcze braki w tej dziedzinie.
– There are still certain shortcomings **in that area**.

Dziwne

I. *'Nic dziwnego, że ...'*

No wonder ... (without **that**)
It is not wonder that ...

II. *'Nic też dziwnego, że ...'*

No wonder, then, that ...
It is hardly surprising, then, that ...
So **it was not surprising that ...**
So **it was no surprise that ...**
So **it's only natural that ...**

Here are some sentences illustrating this phrase:

1. Nic dziwnego, że wiele pierwszych miejsc w tych Igrzyskach zajęli Rosjanie.
– **No wonder** the Russians took so many golds at the Olympics.
– **Small wonder that ...**
– It wasn't surprising that ...

2. Przemyt nasila się, nic dziwnego, że przepisy muszą być zaostrzone.

– Smuggling is on the increase, so it's **small cause for wonder** that the regulations must be tightened up.

3. Prowadzi tak nerwowy tryb życia, że nic dziwnego, iż cierpi na bezsenność.
– His life is so hectic, **it comes as no surprise** that he suffers from insomnia.

4. Jego twórczość była wspaniała, nic więc dziwnego, że zaliczono go do najwybitniejszych malarzy tamtego okresu.
– His paintings were so magnificent that **it's not surprising** he was regarded as one of the most outstanding artists of that period.

5. Nic też dziwnego, że uzyskał poparcie i zaufanie prawie wszystkich wyborców.
– **Little wonder, then, that** he had the support and confidence of nearly all the voters.

6. Pogoda była okropna, nic więc dziwnego, że nie przyszedł.
– The weather was so awful, **it was no surprise** that he didn't come.

Genialny

Here we have a case of two words – English and Polish — looking very much alike. But in fact they have very different meanings.

Note that the Polish word 'genialny' means **exceptionally clever**, whereas the English word **genial**, which looks very similar, has quite a different meaning. **Genial** in English means **kindly, jolly, friendly, good-tempered**.

Główny

'Główny' presents few or no translation problems when used as an adjective accompanying a common noun (i.e. one which begins with a small letter).

Thus we can translate 'główny' as: **chief, foremost, principal, key**, etc. to accompany many different nouns such as: worry, task, problem, architect of sth, inspector, etc., e.g.

my **chief** worry was ...
the **main** problem is not ... but ...
The Prime Minister's **principal** task is to ...
The **key** problem before us is ...

The translation of 'główny' with proper nouns

Most of the aforesaid collocations (links) between common noun and adjective are interchangeable. We can say, for instance: **principal worry, chief task**, etc.

But some difficulties arise when we come to proper nouns – to names of streets, or names of bridges, etc., and especially when the adjective component of the proper name is 'Główny', and when we propose to translate 'Główny' as **Main**.

In Poland, many elements of the country's infrastructure, such as bridges or stations, and many institutions and offices (posts), have names bearing the word 'Główny', e.g. 'Dworzec Główny' (Station), 'Główny Urząd Statystyczny' (Office), etc.

The trouble is that in English the adjectives cited above (key, chief, principal, etc.) are not found as part of proper nouns. The adjective **main**, it is true, is sometimes used in conjunction with a common noun, but with a small letter, e.g. 'You must go along **the main road** (descriptive), and at the traffic lights turn left, into **the High Street** (proper noun)'; we find 'some shops in the **main street**', but never (in British English) 'some shops in **Main Street**'.

Nevertheless we do encounter quite a few combinations with **Central**, e.g. the **Central Station** (Dworzec Centralny). In fact, **Central** is an adjective commonly used with the names of Stations, Committees, Schools, etc. And it would seem to be most appropriate, when translating proper names, to use **Central** as the English equivalent of 'Główny', e.g. 'Dworzec Główny'. In such examples **Central** really means 'Główny'.

1. Główny Urząd Pocztowy znajduje się na skrzyżowaniu ul. Świętokrzyskiej i Marszałkowskiej.

– **The Central Post Office** is at the corner of Świętokrzyska and Marszałkowska Streets.

2. Z Głównego Urzędu Pocztowego Helena nadała telegram do swoich rodziców, zawiadamiając ich, o której godzinie będzie u nich.
– Helena sent a telegram to her parents from the **Central Post Office**, telling them when she would arrive.

When 'Główny' is applied to a station, it would likewise generally be translated as **Central**, eg.

3. Większość pociągów odjeżdża z Dworca Głównego.
– Most trains leave from the **Central Station**.

Note 1: We could leave the name in the original Polish: 'Most trains leave from Dworzec Główny' – that is, the main station. Here, **main** is not part of a proper name, hence the small letter 'm'.

Note 2: We would be unlikely to use the word **Main** (with a capital 'M') as part of a proper name.

In Warsaw, the problem is complicated, by the fact that we have both 'Dworzec Główny' (station no longer used), and 'Dworzec Centralny'. In their time, both meant 'the most important station'.

All in all, we should be inclined to translate both 'Główny' and 'Centralny' here as **Central**. So to distinguish the two, we could use **Central** for the station now known as the 'Centralny', and **former Central** for the 'Główny'.

4. Na Dworcu Głównym w Warszawie utworzono Muzeum Kolejnictwa Polskiego.
– A Polish Railway Museum has been opened in Warsaw's **former Central Station**.

Apart from its use with stations and other buildings, 'Główny', as part of a proper noun, is sometimes translated as **head**. But it is advisable to begin this word with a small letter, not a capital, since in English **Head** is rarely used as part of a name, e.g.

5. Odwołała się w tej sprawie do Głównego Urzędu Ceł.
– She took the matter up with the **head Customs Office**.

6. Główny Komitet Kultury Fizycznej i Turystyki dysponuje funduszami na rozwój sportu w naszym kraju.
– Poland's **Central Committee for Physical Culture and Tourism** manages funds for the development of sport in Poland.

7. Wyniki badań Głównego Urzędu Statystycznego potwierdzają tę tezę.
– Studies carried out by the **Central Statistical Office** confirm this hypothesis.

The translation of 'główny' with common nouns

The translation of 'główny' when used with a common noun is often successfully translated into English as **main** (with a small 'm'), e.g.

1. Głównym celem Wilberforce'a było uwolnienie niewolników.
– Wilberforce's **main aim** was to free the slaves.

In such cases another adequate translation of 'główny' would be **principal** or **foremost**.

Informować

In Polish, this verb can be either transitive or intransitive – often the latter. But the English verb **to inform** is always transitive.

Note the following sentences:

Służba sejsmiczna poinformowała o rychłym niebezpieczeństwie trzęsienia ziemi.
(Note that the Polish verb is intransitive. But in English this verb must have a direct object. So we could say):
– The authorities **informed the public** that there was imminent danger of an earthquake.

Here is another example, showing how we may make the English verb transitive:

Z przykrością informujemy, że od dziś wzrasta cena naszej gazety.
– We regret **to inform our readers** that the price of our paper has gone up from today.

Istotną rzeczą jest ...

Here are several ways of translating the above phrase:

A. 'Istotną rzeczą jest' + rzeczownik

Istotną rzeczą jest wiarygodność wyników.
– Reliability of the results is **very important**.

Note: The best way to translate such a sentence is to turn it round, so that what is important becomes the subject, and appears at the beginning of the sentence, while **is very important** comes at the end.

B. 'Istotną rzeczą jest to, że ...'

Here we will have sentences describing a *factual situation.*
Let us take a simple sentence as an illustration, and give some of the ways in which 'Istotną rzeczą jest to, że ...' can be translated.

Istotną rzeczą jest to, że wszyscy się znamy.
– **The important thing is that** we all know each other.
– **What is important is the fact that ...**
– **The main point is that ...**
– **An important point is the fact that ...**
– **What matters is that ...**
– **What counts is that ...**

C. 'Istotną rzeczą jest to, aby ...' + infinitive; no subject is mentioned

Here the phrase 'Istotną rzeczą jest, aby...' is used to introduce a postulate. Several different constructions may be used in English, e.g.

a) After 'aby' we use an active, affirmative infinitive; no subject is mentioned:

Istotną rzeczą jest to, aby zdawać sobie sprawę z powagi problemu.
– **The important thing is** to recognise the seriousness of the problem.
– **It is very important**...

Similarly:

Istotną rzeczą jest to, aby pamiętać o regularnej konserwacji lodówki.
– **It is essential** to have the fridge serviced regularly.

b) Now we come to similar sentences where 'Istotną rzeczą jest, aby...' is followed by an active, negative infinitive; no subject is mentioned, e.g.

Istotną rzeczą jest to, aby nie hamować postępu w nauce.
– **It is very important not to** hinder scientific progress.

D. 'Istotną rzeczą jest to, aby ...' + subordinate clause

And now to cases where 'Istotną rzeczą jest, aby ...' is followed by a subordinate clause where the subject is mentioned, and where the verb is active, affirmative:

Jest istotną rzeczą, aby proces przebiegał bez wstrząsów.

In translating this, we can use either of two possible constructions. Either we can use **for** + the subject + an active, affirmative infinitive:

– It is **very important for** this process **to take place** smoothly.

Or we can use the verb in the *subjunctive* form to indicate a postulate:

– It is **very important that** this process **take place** smoothly.

Note that **take place** is the subjunctive form of the verb 'take place'.

Analogously there are cases where 'Istotną rzeczą jest, aby ...' is followed by a subordinate clause where the subject is mentioned, and where the verb is in the passive, affirmative form:

> Istotną rzeczą jest to, aby roboty zostały ukończone przed końcem roku.

Again we have two possibilities. Either we can use **for** + the subject + a passive, affirmative verb in the infinitive:

> – It is **very important for** the work **to be completed** before the end of the year.

or we can use the verb in the subjunctive form, to emphasize that a postulate is involved:

> – It is **very important that** the work **be completed** before the end of the year.

Note that **be** is the subjunctive form of **is** or **are**, hence **is completed** becomes **be completed**.

The subjunctive form is the best.

Jeszcze

The Polish word 'jeszcze' has many meanings, and is used in many different kinds of context. Very often it refers to *time*, sometimes it means *more*, or *any more*, in other cases it is used to add *emphasis*, or even to denote *underemphasis*, and sometimes it has *idiomatic meanings.* These meanings are all translated differently, and are discussed below.

The first thing that the translator must do is to be quite clear as to the meaning of the Polish text, which in the case of 'jeszcze' is unfortunately often quite ambiguous. As has been pointed out before, the translator must conjure up the scene evoked by the words in the Polish text, and apply the English commentary to that scene. To repeat, one must translate not the words, but the context they evoke. It is essential to visualise the scene, and verbalise that. One cannot say how one should translate 'jeszcze' without seeing it in context.

Let us examine some of the different ways of translating 'jeszcze'.

I. TIME

Even when 'jeszcze' refers to time alone, its meaning will vary according to the situation, and the translation will vary accordingly. Depending on the context, it may be translated by such different expressions as **still**, **yet**, **even as late as**, **even**, **even as early as**, **even as far back as**, **as long ago as**. But these (often antithetical) expressions are not interchangeable. Let us examine some of them:

a) *'jeszcze' translated as* ***still*** *(expressing continuation):*

In affirmative statements:

Past

1. Mimo że skończyła już czterdzieści parę lat, była jeszcze piękną kobietą.
– Despite her forty-odd years she was **still** a beautiful woman.

Present

2. On kocha ją jeszcze.
– He **still** loves her.

Future

3. Jeszcze będziemy mogli się widywać.
– We'll **still** be able to see each other.

In interrogative statements:

Past

4. Czy w czasie twego pobytu tam wojna jeszcze trwała?
– Was the war **still** going on when you were there?

Present

5. Czy kochasz mnie jeszcze?
– Do you **still** love me?

Future

6. Czy będziesz jeszcze w domu, gdy ona przyjdzie?
– Will you **still** be at home when she comes?

In negative statements:

b) *'jeszcze nie' translated as* ***not yet*** *(expressing the idea of not having reached some point of reference):*

Past

7. Nie przyszedł jeszcze.
– He's **not** here **yet**.
(See below, compare – **still not**).

Present

8. Jeszcze nie dostajesz tych książek.
– You're **not** getting these books **yet**.

Future

9. Jeszcze długo nie zrozumiesz swego błędu.
– It **will be a long time before** you understand your mistake.

c) *'jeszcze nie' translated as* ***still not*** (*continuation of a negative state*):

10. Jeszcze nie doszła do siebie.
– She **still hasn't** recovered.

d) *Differences between* ***still*** and ***yet***:

In the first place, **still** is generally used in affirmative statements. **Not yet** is used only in negative statements.

e) *The difference between* ***not yet*** and ***still not*** *may be illustrated by some more examples:*

11. Moje buty jeszcze nie są gotowe.
– My boots aren't ready **yet**. (neutral statement of fact; expression of time only, not mood)
– My boots **still** are**n't** ready. (this translation expresses impatience, disappointment of expectations; it expresses not only time, but mood as well)

12. Już czwarta, a jego jeszcze nie ma.
– It's four o'clock and he's **not** here **yet**. (bare statement of fact; little emphasis on mood)

– It's four o'clock already, and he's **still not** here! (statement of fact, and indication of mood; the meaning is: 'We've been expecting him; he should be here by now'; mood of annoyance; in spoken English the word **still** is stressed.)

f) *Moreover, in sentences with 'jeszcze nie' there is quite often ambiguity in the Polish text. Consider the following examples:*

13. Wciąż jeszcze nie wiem, gdzie będę pracował.
This could be translated in two different ways, depending on the meaning:
– I do**n't** know **yet** where I'm going to work. (factual, neutral statement)
– I **still** do**n't** know where I'm going to work. (I've been thinking about it for a long time, and haven't decided yet; emphasis on length of decision-making; **still** = 'nadal'. Note the position of **yet** and **still** in relation to the verb; **yet** comes after the subject and the verb; **still** comes after the subject and before the verb.)

g) *'jeszcze' translated as* ***as early as, as late as, as far back as, as long as:***

Here, too, difficulties are caused by occasional ambiguity in the Polish text. The translator must simply use his own judgement, and guess at the meaning:

14. Domy te, zbudowane może jeszcze przez osadników holenderskich, są bardzo piękne.
– These houses, perhaps **dating back** to the time of the Dutch settlers, are very beautiful.

Ambiguity is even more marked in the following sentence:

15. Jeszcze w roku 1849 ostrzegano go, że może w ten sposób stracić majątek.
It is not clear from the Polish text whether this means **as early as**, or **as late as**. Several translations are possible:
– In 1849 he was **still** being warned that he could lose his estate that way.
– **Even as late as** 1849 he was (**still** being) warned ...

– **Even as early as** 1849 he was warned ...
– **Even as far back** as 1849 he was warned ...
– **Even as long ago as** 1849 he was warned ...

Note the use of the word **even**, which adds emphasis to the above phrases.

h) *Now see 'jeszcze' in conjunction with adverbs of time, e.g. 'jeszcze raz', 'jeszcze nieraz' (repetition):*

16. Zagraj to jeszcze raz!
– Play it **again** / Play it **once more!**

17. Jeszcze nieraz (past) widziałem go pijanego.
– Later on, I saw him drunk **on a number of occasions / many a time.**

Sometimes we use an idiomatic translation of 'jeszcze nieraz' (future):

18. Jeszcze nieraz odczujemy skutki jego wybryków.
– This won't be **the last time** we'll have to suffer the consequences of his goings-on.

II. JESZCZE MEANING 'MORE' OR 'ANYTHING/SOMETHING ELSE'

a) *'Jeszcze' meaning* **more** *(with regard to number or quantity):*

19. Daj mi jeszcze trochę.
– Give me a little more!

20. Poproszę jeszcze dwa!
– Two more, please!

b) *'Jeszcze' in conjunction with 'ktoś' or 'coś':*

21. Ktoś jeszcze ma przyjść.
– **Someone else** is meant to be coming.

22. Nie wiem, czy przyjdzie ktoś jeszcze.
– I don't know if **anyone else** will come.

Similarly: 'coś jeszcze' – **anything else; something else**

23. Zjesz coś jeszcze?
– Will you have **something else** (to eat)?

24. Czy mogę dla Ciebie coś zrobić jeszcze?
– Can I do **anything else** for you?

III. EMPHASIS

If 'jeszcze' is used with comparatives to add emphasis, it can be translated by **even**, or **still**, or **...than ever**:

25. Wspólne nieszczęście zbliżyło ich jeszcze bardziej.
– Their common misfortune brought them **even** closer together / **still** closer together / closer together **than ever**.

26. Trudno w takim świecie żyć, jeszcze trudniej osiągnąć w nim szczęście.
– It is difficult to live in such a world, and **even more difficult** / and **more difficult still** to achieve happiness.

Still in such cases often comes after the word it qualifies. This inversion strengthens the emphasis.

Another example shows how inversion of the word order strengthens emphasis:

27. Jeszcze takich owacji w życiu nie słyszałem!
Compare:
– I've never in my life heard such applause. (normal order)
– Never in my life have I heard such applause. (inversion of the word order makes the emphasis stronger)

IV. UNDEREMPHASIS

Sometimes we can use the words **not so very...** to express underemphasis:

28. Stało się to jeszcze nie tak dawno.
– It happened **not so very long** ago.

V. IDIOMATIC TRANSLATIONS OF 'JESZCZE'

Quite often the use of 'jeszcze' calls for a more idiomatic translation into English:

29. Jeszcze tego brakowało żeby przyszli na święta!
– If they came for Christmas, that would **put the lid on it! / it would be just about the limit! / it would be the absolute end! / it would be just about the last straw! / that would just about crown it!**

One or two more idiomatic or slang translations are given below.

30. Dobrze bawiliście się?
– Did you have a good time?
Jeszcze jak!
– **I should say! / You bet! / Bet your life we did! / Not half! We sure did! / And how!**

31. Czy ona podoba Ci się?
Jeszcze jak!
– Do you like her?
– And how!
– What do you think of her?
– Wow!
– Do you think she's pretty?
– I sure do! Yes, I do!
– You bet I do!

'Jeszcze' sometimes means **even**:

Comparative adjective
Jej siostra jest ładna, ale Ewa jeszcze ładniejsza.
– Her sister is good-looking, but Eve is **even** prettier.

Comparative adverb
Samochód jechał z prędkością 80 km na godzinę, lecz pociąg jeszcze szybciej.
– The car was doing 80, but the train was going **even** faster.

32. To jeszcze gorzej niż przedtem.
– It's **even** worse than before.

*

33. **Any more?**
Czy są jakieś ciasteczka jeszcze?
– Are there **any more** cakes?

34. **Any left?**
Czy są truskawki jeszcze?
– Are there **any** strawberries **left?**

Już

I. TIME

Probably 'już' is used most often to indicate *time.*

a) *'już' referring to the future:*

The translation may be idiomatic:

1. Kiedy on przyjdzie?
Już niedługo.
– When will he be here?
– It won't be long **now**.

Translate 'już nigdy' (referring to the future) as: **never again**:

2. Przypuszczam, że go już nigdy nie zobaczę.
– I suppose I'll **never** see him **again**.
(Note the word order!)

b) 'już' *referring to the present:*

The translation will depend on how the translator interprets the Polish text, and how he imagines the context:

3. Która godzina?
Już czwarta.
– What time is it?
– It's four o'clock **already**.

4. Jest już za późno, aby płakać nad swoim losem.
- It's too late **in the day** to cry over your fate now.
- It's too late **now** to cry over your fate.
- It's **far** too late to cry over your fate now.
- It's too late to cry over your fate **now**.

Note the position of **now** – it can come either after **late**, or at the end of the sentence.

5. Już od czasu tej choroby jest bardzo słaby.
- **Ever** since that illness, he **has been** very weak. (note the perfect tense)

6. Budynek ten już dziś wymaga kapitalnego remontu. (= as early as at the present day = so soon)
- The building is **now** badly in need of major repairs.
- The building is **already** badly in need of major repairs.

Note that here 'już' qualifies the adverb of time 'dziś', not the verb 'wymaga'.

7. Tak więc wiemy już, co to znaczy.
- So **now** we know what it means.
- So we know **now** what it means.
- So we **already** know what it means.

c) *'już' referring to the past:*

8. W końcu dowiedzieliśmy się już, co to znaczy.
- **In the end** we learned what it meant.

9. Już przedtem wiedzieliśmy, co to znaczy.
- We knew **by then** what it meant.
- We **already** knew what it meant.
- We knew **before then** what it meant.
- We knew **beforehand** what it meant.

10. Zdołaliśmy już go poznać.
This sentence can be interpreted in many different ways:

– We had had an opportunity to make his acquaintance **beforehand**.
– We had **already** managed to make his acquaintance.
– We know **now** what he's like.
– We know **by now** what he's like.
– We've had **enough** time to find out what he's like.
– We've **already** had an opportunity to find out what he's like.
– We've managed **already** to find out what he's like.
– We had **already** found out what he was like.
– We'd had time **enough** to find out what he was really like.

Note the tenses. Note, too, the tense where a past process is still going on.

11. Po kilku minutach rozmawiali już jak starzy znajomi.
– After **only** a few minutes they were talking together like old friends.
– After a few minutes they were **already** talking ...
– In **less than** five minutes they were talking ...
– It was only a few minutes **before** they were talking ...
– **No more than** a few minutes had passed before they were talking ...
– After a couple of minutes they were **already** talking ...

Note that the meaning is: 'już po kilku minutach'. *Note* also the use of the past continuous tense in English.

12. Już w latach siedemdziesiątych złotnictwo warszawskie uległo wpływom sztuki klasycystycznej.
– **By** the seventies, the work of Warsaw goldsmiths **was already** coming under (or: had **already** begun to come under) the influence of the neo-classical style in art.

Note the use of **by** + the past continuous tense or the pluperfect tense, depending on the meaning, and also the use of **already**, which should be placed next to the verb, between the auxiliary and the participle.

In the next sentence, 'już' means **just about to, on the point of**. Again we can use the past continuous tense.

13. Już mieliśmy wyjść, kiedy zaczął padać deszcz.
– We were **just** going out when it began to rain.
– When we were **about to** go out, it began to rain.
– We were **just about to** go out, when it began to rain.
– We were **on the point of** going out, when it began to rain.
– As we were **about to** go out, it began to rain.

Note the construction **for** + the perfect tense:

14. Już od pięciu lat notuje się bardzo dynamiczny wzrost produkcji.
– **For** the **last** five years there has been a very dynamic increase in production.
– **For** five years **now** there has been ...

This tense in English denotes that the process is still going on. Compare this with the following sentences:

15. Minęło już pięć lat, kiedy go zobaczyłem po raz ostatni.
– Five years **have** passed **since** I saw him last.

The meaning of 'już' here is conveyed by the use of the perfect tense.

16. Już pięć lat temu wiedziałem co będzie.
– Even **as far back as** five years ago, I knew what would happen.
– Even **as long as** five years ago, ...

In another case where the perfect tense is used, it occurs in conjunction with **already**.

17. W poprzedniej części książki posługiwaliśmy się już terminem 'lingwistyka stosowana'.
– The term 'applied linguistics' has **already** been used in a previous section of this book.

Note the position of **already** – between the auxiliary verb and the past participle (not emphasized). If we wished to emphasize **already**, we would put it at the end of the sentence:

'The term ... has been used in a previous section of the book **already**'. or after the past participle: '... has been used **already** in a previous section of the book'.

d) *'już' + the negative:*

'Już' may be translated by **no ... any more, no ... left, no longer, nothing more, all ... gone**.

18. Nie było już żadnego ratunku.
– **All** hope was **gone**.
– There was **no longer** any hope.
– There was **no** hope of rescue **any more**.
– **Nothing more** could be done.

19. Nie było już chleba.
– There was **no** bread **left**. (none ... left)
Nie kocham cię już.
– I **don't** love you **any more**.

e) *'już' in questions:*

The meaning of 'już' may vary. If it means **now**, we may translate 'już' by **yet:**

20. Czy już odrobiłeś lekcje?
– Have you finished your lessons **yet?**

21. Czy już skończyłeś tę książkę?
– Have you finished the book **yet**?

But if it means **beforehand**, we may use **already** with the perfect tense, or **before** with the pluperfect tense:

22. Czy czytałeś już tę książkę?
– Have you read this book **already**?
– Had you read the book **before**?

Whether we use **yet**, or on the other hand **before**, or **already**, will depend on the point from which the speaker views the situation.

II. EMPHASIS

a) *Sometimes 'już' is used for emphasis, not time e.g.:*

1. Pomijając już to, że praca nie została wykonana na czas, została wykonana źle.
– **In addition to** the work's not having been done on time, it was done badly.
– **Even despite** the fact that ...
– **Even** leaving aside the fact that ...
– **Even** disregarding the fact that ...
– **Even though** the work was not done on time ...
– **Quite apart** from the fact that ...

(= in addition to other considerations)

b) *Sometimes 'już' has no exact equivalent in English, as we see from the following sentences:*

The translation may have to be idiomatic in which case it will depend on the interpretation of the context, e.g.

2. Przestań marudzić! Zjedz to już wreszcie!
– Stop dawdling over your food. Get on with it!

3. Uciekaj, ale już! (exasperation)
– Beat it! Scram, right now!
(mother to child):
– Out!
– (Be) off with you!
– Run along now! Quick!

(to prisoner):
– Get out of here, and be quick about it!
– Get out, and make it fast!
– Get going while the going's good!

There may be no indication of 'już' in the English sentence at all:

4. Ja już się z nim rozprawię, jak go złapię!
– I'll teach him a lesson, when I get my hands on him!

c) *Emphasis to express something unexpected:*

5. Ledwie wyszedł ze szpitala, a już znalazł się tam znowu.
– Hardly had he got out of hospital, when he landed back in there again.

There is nothing in the English sentence that really conveys the meaning of 'już', except perhaps the inverted word order at the beginning of the sentence.

d) *Mixed examples:*

TIME + EMPHASIS: 'już' + negative

6. Nigdy już tam nie pójdę po tym, co Andrzej mi powiedział.
– I'll never go there **again**, after what Andrew told me.
– I won't ever go there **again**, after ...
– I won't go there **any more**, after ...

Thus we can translate 'nigdy już' as: **never again, not ever again, not any more, never any more, never / ever ... any more**

EMPHASIS + TIME + EMOTION (here, exasperation)

7. Już po raz drugi popełnili ten sam błąd.
– That's the second time they've made the same mistake.

– They've gone and made the same mistake again.

Note the construction: 'That's the ...'

III. EMOTIONAL ATTITUDE

The translation may be purely idiomatic, based on visualization of the context.

a) *Exasperation:*

8. (Znowu spóźnili się na obiad!) Tego już za wiele!
- I've had **just enough**!
- I've had **just about enough**!
- No, this is **too much**!
- That **does it**!
- That's a bit **too much**!
- That's **just the limit**!
- That's the **last straw**!
- That's **too much**, really!
- That's **the limit**!

b) *Relief, reassurance:*

9. (Proszę się uspokoić), już po wszystkim!
- It's all **over** now. (= you can relax)
- That's it, it's **finished**.
- It's all **behind** us now.
- All our troubles are **over** now.
- No need to worry **now**!

The translation will depend on the context. It is essential to visualize the scene in which these words are used. A mechanical, word-for-word translation, is unlikely to be of much use.

c) *Despair at something being over:*

The translation will depend on the context again.

10. Już koniec, po wszystkim!
– This is the end! We're finished! (e.g. ship sinking)
– That's us finished. There's no hope. (e.g. miners trapped in a pit)
– That's it. We've had it. (e.g. soldiers in a desperate situation)
– It's all over. And that's that. (e.g. end of a love affair)

IV. READINESS (IDIOMATIC TRANSLATION)

11. 'Już?'
– **Ready?** (e.g. to go for a walk)
– Are you **ready**? Is it **ready**? etc.
– **Finished**? (e.g. mother to child eating breakfast)
– All **done**? (e.g. teacher asking if all the pupils in her class have finished a test)
– **Done**? (e.g. teacher to pupils)
– Have you drunk it **all up**? (mother to child)
– Have you eaten **all** your dinner? (e.g. mother to child)

Kamienica

This is a difficult word to translate. It is not always absolutely clear what kind of building is termed a 'kamienica'. Originally, as its Polish name indicates, it was one built of stone or brick. The picture conveyed by the Polish word is that of a fairly large building on several floors, containing a number of independent units let out to tenants. Thus it is a multiple occupancy structure.

A number of sentences in which 'kamienica' is translated from Polish into English are given below.

1. Kamienica, w której znajduje się winiarnia, należała kiedyś do rodziny Fukierów.
– This **stone building**, now a wine-bar, once belonged to the Fukier family.

2. Doktor wynajmował skromny pokój na parterze w ponurej kamienicy na Długiej.
– The doctor rented a modest ground-floor room in a gloomy **tenement** in Długa Street.

3. Dom nr 7 przy ulicy Zielonej był trzypiętrową kamienicą czynszową.
– No. 7 Green Street was a three-storey building with flats let out to various tenants and was thus classed as a **tenement**.

4. W tej kamienicy mieszkali przed wojną moi rodzice.
– Before the war, my parents lived in that **building**.

5. Wśród wielu kamienic Starówki szczególnym pięknem wyróżnia się kamienica Fukierów.
– Among the many **historic houses** in the Old Town, the one that belonged to the Fukier family is particularly beautiful.

6. Nasza kuzynka mieszka od lat w tej samej starej kamienicy.
– Our cousin has lived for years in the same old **tenement building**.

7. Przy ulicy Noakowskiego stoi kilka kamienic w stylu secesyjnym.
– Noakowskiego Street has several art nouveau style buildings.

Here are some other sentences, where houses are named:

8. W tzw. kamienicy Krauzowskiej jest portal kamienny z poł. XVII w.
– The Krauze **tenement** has a stone portal dating from the middle of the 17th cent.

9. Kamienica nr 20 należała do H. Kołłątaja.
– The **building** at No. 20 once belonged to Kołłątaj.

10. Pod nr 6 przy Rynku stoi 'Szara Kamienica' rzekomo zbudowana przez Kazimierza Wielkiego.
– At No. 6 in the Market Square is the **Grey House**, said to have been built by Kazimierz the Great.

11. Pod nr 17 mieści się 'kamienica Hetmańska', o gotyckich sklepieniach.
– At No. 17 is **Hetman House**, with its Gothic vaulting.

12. Pałac Pod Baranami powstał z połączenia 3 kamienic.
– At the Sign of the Sheep, the Pod Baranami **mansion** was created by joining three houses together.

The best general translation to use for 'kamienica' is **building**.

Kilka

The Polish word 'kilka' has several equivalents, or near-equivalents, in English: **several, some, a few**, as may be seen in the following sentences:

1. Czy mógłbyś pójść ze mną do teatru dziś wieczór?
Przykro mi, ale nie mogę, to przyjdzie do nas kilka osób na kolację.
– Can you come to the theatre with me this evening?
– I'm sorry, I can't. We have **some** people coming to dinner.

2. Czy znasz kogoś w Krakowie?
Tak, znam kilka osób.
– Do you know anybody in Cracow?
– Yes, I know **several** people there.

3. Tak, mam tam kilku przyjaciół.
– Yes, I have **some** friends there.

4. Kilka / parę osób obecnych u was znałem już przedtem.
– **Several / some** of the people present at your place were known to me already.

Note: **several** – a few; more than two or three, but not many; **some** – a certain quantity or number.

Kilkadziesiąt

The Polish word 'kilkadziesiąt' has no exact equivalent in English.

The Poles and the English sometimes have different ways of counting things (see also *KILKANAŚCIE*).

Poles will ask for 'dziesięć jajek' (ten eggs), whereas the English will ask for a dozen (or half-dozen). Poles are inclined to count things in tens. They ask for 'dziesięć róż' (ten roses), whereas an Englishman will ask for a dozen (twelve) or a half-dozen. A Pole will ask for ten cakes, whereas an Englishman will be more likely to ask for a dozen (or half-a-dozen) cakes. See *KILKANAŚCIE* on things which in English are counted in dozens (e.g. certain kinds of flowers and fruit, some household things and articles of personal clothing. Some other things, however, are counted by the English in tens, e.g. money (particularly after Britain changed to a decimal currency), but also degrees of temperature, percentages, etc. See also below how duration of time, age, and prison sentences (number of days, minutes, years) are expressed in the two languages. Likewise numbers of people.

The reader will also find at the end of the article on 'kilkanaście' some guidance as to the presence or absence of the word **of** between the numeral and the noun that is counted.

Kilkanaście

'Kilkanaście' is a word which is impossible to translate well into English in every case. For the most part one can only attempt an approximation.

The first thing one must do is to note what is being counted, for on that will depend the translation of 'kilkanaście'.

A. DOZENS

With things that in English can be counted in dozens, but not with others, we can use such phrases as **more than a dozen**, or **a dozen or so**. But note that there are differences between how the Poles and the English count things. In Poland people buy 'pięć goździków', in Britain half-a--dozen carnations. British people buy a dozen eggs, whereas Poles buy 'dziesięć jajek' (ten eggs), etc. This is reflected in the language. There is no exact English equivalent of 'kilkanaście'. The most we can say is that in English *some* things can be counted in dozens, and in these cases it is handy to use a variant of the word **dozen** for 'kilkanaście'.

Things which in English can be counted in dozens:

a) oranges, bananas (not apples, plums, strawberries, etc., which are only bought by weight, not by number)

b) bottles of something (e.g. lemonade, wine)

c) people

d) roses, carnations, etc. (i.e. rather more formal, expensive flowers bought at the florist's; other less formal flowers, such as snowdrops, violets, sweet peas, etc., would be bought in a **bunch**, although the word **bunch** gives no indication of number; we can also say '**a bunch** of roses, carnations, etc.' again not indicating number)

e) household things: plates, saucers, cups, knives, forks, spoons, napkins (serwetki lniane), sheets, pillow-cases, towels

f) personal clothing: shirts, handkerchiefs, etc.

g) pencils

h) tables (e.g. in a restaurant)

i) books.

Examples are given below.

Note 1. Do not use the preposition **of** after **dozen**, e.g.

WRONG – a dozen of people

RIGHT – **a dozen** people, **a dozen** eggs, etc.

Note 2. 'Zaledwie kilkanaście' = barely a dozen.

B. MONEY

One can use **about ten or twenty**, or **over ten**, e.g.

kilkanaście złotych – **about ten or twenty** zlotys

kilkanaście tysięcy złotych – **over ten** thousand zlotys

C. DEGREES OF TEMPERATURE

kilkanaście stopni mrozu

– **over ten** degrees of frost / degrees below / below zero

D. PER CENT

kilkanaście procent

– **between ten and twenty** per cent

Sometimes, (when the meaning is: **exceeding ten**), one can use the phrase **double figures**, e.g.

– Inflation has reached **double figures** again.

E. TIME

1) Years

a) Duration

kilkanaście lat

– **more than a decade, more than ten** years, **about fifteen or twenty** years, etc.

b) Age – Use the word **teens**, e.g.

mieć kilkanaście lat – **be** in one's **teens**

Chłopiec miał kilkanaście lat – The boy **was** in his **teens**.

Młodzieniec – **teen**ager, a youth.

2) Months

a) Duration. Try to express 'kilkanaście miesięcy' in terms of a year, e.g.

kilkanaście miesięcy

– for **about a year**, for **more than a year**, for **about a year and a half**, for **nearly two years**

b) Age. We can either translate the phrase as an approximation in terms of a year, or as a number of months, e.g.

we can describe a baby's age as being: **about a year and a half, just over a year, nearly two years** etc., or **around eighteen months, about fifteen months**, etc.

c) Prison sentences. These are generally expressed as a number of months, e.g.

Był skazany na kilkanaście miesięcy więzienia.

– He was sentenced to **fifteen** months or so in jail.

3) Days

kilkanaście dni

– **about a fortnight / about two weeks**

4) Minutes

kilkanaście minut

– **about a quarter of an hour, about quarter of an hour, quarter of an hour or so**

The above patterns are illustrated by the following examples.

1. Kilkanaście lat temu problem ten nigdy by nie powstał.
– **Ten or twenty years ago** that problem would never have arisen.

2. Nasza grupa liczy kilkunastu studentów.
– There are **about a dozen** students in our group. (Note the plural form of the verb.)

3. Jest kilkanaście stopni mrozu.
– It's **more than ten** degrees below zero.

4. Było zaledwie kilkanaście osób na pogrzebie.
– There were **barely a dozen** people at the funeral.

5. Miała wtedy kilkanaście lat.
– She **was** in her **teens** at the time.

6. Przez kilkanaście minut źle się czułem.
– I felt ill for **quarter of an hour or so**.

7. Mam tylko kilkanaście złotych przy sobie.
– I've only **ten or twenty** zlotys on me.

8. Przez kilkanaście dni w ogóle go nie widziałem.
– For **about a fortnight** I didn't saw him at all.

9. Oczekuje się, że wzrost ceny ropy naftowej może wynieść kilkanaście procent.
– It is expected that oil prices may rise by **between ten and twenty** per cent.

10. Ile osób zaprosiłeś na przyjęcie? – Kilkanaście.
How many people have you asked to the party? – **About a dozen.**

Note that **a few** is not a suitable translation of 'kilkanaście'. 'Kilkanaście' is more than **a few**. Likewise **some** is not a suitable equivalent, as it only means **a number of** (vague).

RIGHT AND WRONG

'kilkanaście lat temu'

WRONG – **A decade and a few** years ago. (This is too clumsy.)
– **Some dozen** years ago. (It is not clear what **some dozen** means, if anything.)
– **About two decades** ago.

RIGHT – A decade or so ago. (not very good)
– **A couple of decades** ago. (better that the sentence above, but too long a period)
– **Ten or fifteen years** ago.

'kilkanaście osób'

WRONG – **Some dozen** people. (It is doubtful if one can say **some dozen** in English at all.)
– **More than ten** people. (This is not a neutral statement like 'kilkanaście', but expresses surprise that there were so many, so the meaning is somewhat distorted.)
– **Only a dozen** people. (This would mean exactly a dozen; moreover, **only** here is an emotive word, expressing regret that there were so few people; this again somewhat distorts the meaning of the Polish text; see **barely a dozen** below.)
– **About a dozen or so** people. (There we have tautology. **About** means the same as **or so**. We would use either **about**, or **or so**, but not both.)
– **Not more than twenty** people; **close on twenty** people, **less than twenty** people, **fewer than twenty**. (All these phrases distort the meaning. 'Kilkanaście' gives no indication as to whether the number in mind is nearer ten or nearer twenty. Moreover, 'kilkanaście' is neutral in tone, whereas all these phrases imply some attitude to the number – e.g. approval or disapproval.)
– **Only a handful** of people. (This means less than 'kilkanaście')
– **Not many** people. (Too vague)
– **A score** of people. (Too many, because **a score** means exactly twenty.)
– **A few**; **quite a few**. (This means a very much smaller number than 'kilkanaście'.)
– **From ten to twenty** people.

POSSIBLE – **Between ten and twenty** people.

RIGHT – **About a dozen** people. (This is the best version.)

Note 3. Do not use the phrase **a dozen or so** too often. It has low frequency in English. Use other phrases with **dozen** (See A, p. 69). But **about a dozen** seems to be the best translation.

'kilkanaście książek'

WRONG – **Ten to twenty** books.
RIGHT – **Ten or twenty** books. (not very good)
– **A dozen or so** books. (slightly better, but still not very good)
– **About a dozen** books. (best version)

'kilkanaście minut'

WRONG – For **some** minutes. (This would mean four or five, certainly less than ten.)
– For **over ten** minutes; for **more than ten** minutes. (This is too precise; 'kilkanaście' is more vague.)
– For **some dozen** minutes. (An impossible construction in English.)
RIGHT – For **about a quarter of an hour**.

'kilkanaście stopni' (*temperature*)

WRONG – **A dozen or so** degrees. (Degrees of temperature are not reckoned by the dozen.)
RIGHT – **More than ten** degrees.

'kilkanaście złotych'

WRONG – **A dozen or so** zlotys. (Zlotys are not reckoned in dozens.)
– **Only a few** zlotys. (This amount is less than ten.)
NOT VERY GOOD – **Not more than twenty** zlotys.
POSSIBLE – **Some small change**. (But this might amount to less than ten.)
RIGHT – **About ten or twenty** zlotys.

'kilkanaście dni'

WRONG – For **several** days. (**Several** means much fewer than 'kilkanaście' – possibly between three and five.)

RIGHT – For **about a fortnight**

AVOID – too frequent use of the words **or so**: e.g. **a fortnight or so**. It is better to use **about**.

'kilkanaście procent'

WRONG – **A dozen or so** per cent. (Do not use the word **dozen** with per cent.)

POSSIBLE – **About fifteen** per cent
– **Some 15%; some 14%**, etc.
– **Over ten** per cent; **more than ten** per cent

Note. None of these are satisfactory. It is impossible to translate such examples properly unless we have a more precise idea of the number which is meant.

'kilkanaście tysięcy'

WRONG – **A few** thousand. (Too little – this would mean three or four.)
– **A couple of** thousand. (Too little – this means two.)
– **Almost twenty** thousand. (Inaccurate – the number indicated might be nearer ten than twenty thousand.)

POSSIBLE – **Over ten** thousand.

Koncentrować

There are only certain things that one can **concentrate:**

a) **concentrate** as a transitive verb,

We can **concentrate** our *efforts*, our *attention*, our *mind*, our *thoughts* and our *ideas* (the verb 'skupiać' is used in the same way: skupiać uwagę, skupiać myśli).

b) **concentrate** as an intransitive verb, e.g.

– **Concentrate** on what you're doing!

c) 'koncentrować' can also be used as a transitive verb in the sense of 'gromadzić', esp. military forces, e.g.

Napoleon koncentrował swoje wojska na terenach położonych wyżej.
– Napoleon **concentrated** his forces on the high ground.

d) Similarly, we can turn this round into the passive form e.g.

– The French forces **were concentrated** on the high ground.
– Nearly 50% of Poland's industrial manpower **was concentrated** in the fuel, textile, and food industries.

In fact the passive form of this verb is more common than the active.

Kraj

This word has a very much higher frequency among the Poles than its presumed equivalent among English-speaking people.

Whereas Poles would say:

Po czternastu latach spędzonych w Afryce równikowej Jurek z ochotą wrócił do kraju (without mentioning the name of their home country – Poland),

British people would be more likely to say:

– After fourteen years in equatorial Africa, George was glad to get back to **Britain** (i.e. mentioning the name **Britain**).

Possibly this difference results from the fact that the English language does not have a word exactly corresponding in emotional force to 'kraj', which has all sorts of overtones.

On the other hand, British people who had been living in India, or similar regions, might perhaps use the word **home**, or **the home country**, in this kind of situation.

Krajowy

Whereas the Poles normally use 'krajowy' as an adjective instead of 'polski' (e.g. 'duże krajowe drapieżniki' meaning **large Polish predators**), English people often use the noun form **home** as an adjective, as in: **home-produced tomatoes, home produce, home-cured ham**, although they also use the specific adjectives referring to country of origin, e.g. **Scotch salmon, English tomatoes**, etc.

Leżący u podstaw ...

It is hoped that the following examples of translation of the above phrase will be self-explanatory.

I. *Założenia leżące u podstaw czegoś pozytywnego*

Założenia leżące u podstaw naszego ustawodawstwa ...
– The **principles underlying** Britain's legislation ...
– The **principles forming the basis of** our legislation ...
– The **principles behind** our legislation ...
– The **principles constituting the foundation of** our legislation ...

Założenie (zasada) leżące u podstaw teorii Einsteina głosi, że ...
– The **principle underlying** Einstein's theory is that ...
– The **principle upon which** Einstein's theory **is based** assumes that ...
– The **principle forming the basis of** Einstein's theory states that ...

II. *Założenia leżące u podstaw czegoś negatywnego*

Przyczyny leżące u podstaw naszych niepowodzeń gospodarczych to ...
– The **reasons underlying** our economic ills are ...
– The **factors responsible for** our economic ills are ...
– The **roots of** our economic ills lie in ...

Liczy sobie ... lat

It is hoped that here, too, the difference between right and wrong translation is clear:

1. Nasz Instytut liczy sobie 15 lat.
WRONG – Our Institute **numbers** 15 years,
RIGHT – Our Institute **is 15 years old**.

2. Ten sławny obraz, ukazujący króla i jego rodzinę, liczy sobie 350 lat.
WRONG – This famous picture, showing the king and his family, **numbers 350 years**.
WRONG – This famous picture, showing the king and his family, **is 350 years of age**.
RIGHT – This famous picture, showing the king and his family, **is 350 years old**.

3. Sprawa zniknięcia brązowego orła liczy już 9 lat.
WRONG – The case of the disappearance of the bronze eagle already **counts nine years**.
RIGHT – The case of the disappearance of the bronze eagle **has been open for nine years.**
RIGHT – The case of the bronze eagle **remains unsolved** after nine years.

Clearly this phrase shows that the English language construction is quite different from that of the Polish.

Lokalnie

'Lokalnie' is a Polish adverb very similar in appearance to the English adverb **locally**, but it often has rather a different meaning. Whereas the English adverb **locally** means *confined to the place we are talking about*, the Polish adverb 'lokalnie' often means *occurring in particular areas, different, various areas.*

Note the following examples of translation:

1. Wyziewy kominów fabrycznych zmieniają lokalnie chemiczny skład powietrza.
   – The smoke coming from the factory chimneys has been poisoning the air **in these areas**.

2. Lokalnie, zwłaszcza na południu kraju, wystąpią mgły i zamglenia.
   – There will be **pockets** of mist and fog, especially in the south.
   – There will be **local** mist and fog, especially in parts of the south.

3. Lokalnie należy oczekiwać deszczu i zamglenia.
   – Rain and mist are expected **in some places**.

4. Lokalnie na drogach wystąpi gołoledź.
   – **Here and there** road surfaces will be icy.

5. Jutro lokalnie na południu wystąpią burze.
   – Thunderstorms will occur tomorrow **in some** southern **areas**.

6. Dziś w nocy na terenie kraju lokalnie występowały przymrozki.
   – Last night there was ground frost **in some parts of Poland**.

Note. Locally should not be used as an English adverb corresponding to the Polish ‘lokalnie’. As we have seen, these two words do not always correspond to each other in meaning.

Machnąć ręką (na coś)

The gesture referred to in this phrase is one of annoyance, resignation, impatience, indifference, dismissal, rejection of something done or said by another person, or determination to ignore something said. When someone makes this gesture, he brings one hand down sharply and outwards, palm down, as if pushing away what the other person has said. It is a physical gesture, common in Poland but practically unknown in Britain. But even without the physical gesture, the metaphorical meaning remains.

Different nationalities use different forms of body language. As we have said, the gesture referred to in Polish as ‘machnąć ręką na coś’ scarcely exists among British people. ‘Machnąć ręką’ may indeed correspond to a similar mental attitude, but to quite a different British body gesture, expressed in the phrase **to shrug one's shoulders**, implying similar emotions of impatience, indifference, dismissal, rejection of something another person has said or done. If, when translating, one considers the mental attitude to be just as important, or more important, than the physical gesture, it might well be permissible, and even advisable, to translate 'machnąć ręką' as **shrug one's shoulders**, e.g.

– Mąż machnął ręką na wybryki syna.
– The husband **shrugged his shoulders** on hearing of his son's escapades.

Only once has the present writer encountered in her reading an English equivalent of the Polish 'machnąć ręką'. This was: **he made a dismissive gesture**, and was encountered in one of books in Anthony Powell's *Music of Time* series.

Miejscami

The following translations may be regarded as adequate.

1. Las miejscami był bardzo gęsty.
– The forest was very dense **in places**.

2. Miejscami widać jeszcze pozostałości wojny.
– **Here and there** you can still see the scars of war.

3. Teren tu jest przeważnie płaski, a tylko miejscami pagórkowaty.
– The land here is mostly flat, only **in places** is it hilly.

4. W wysokich partiach gór rosną miejscami szarotki.
– **Sometimes** edelweiss can be found in the higher parts of the Alps.

5. Na nowej linii pociągi będą mogły miejscami rozwijać prędkość nawet do 250 km na godzinę.
– **On some sections** of the new line trains will be able to travel at speeds of up to 250 km per hour.

6. Na terenie Lubelszczyzny miejscami występuje siarka.
– **In some parts** of the Lublin region, sulphur occurs.

Thus, possible translations of 'miejscami' are: **in places, sometimes, here and there, on some sections** of sth, **in some parts** of sth.

M.in. (między innymi) (literally = among other things)

Instead of translating this abbreviations as **among others**, as is commonly done, it is often better to use the word **including**, e.g.

Konsekwencją tego było uznanie nowego suwerennego państwa, Bangladesz, przez wiele krajów, m.in. Polskę.
– The result was that the new sovereign state, Bangladesh, was recognised by many countries, **including** Poland.

Młody

Note the various tricky points in these translations:

1. To młody, obiecujący pisarz.
– He's a **promising young** writer.
(Note the order in English of the two adjectives, **young** comes second, after **promising**.)

2. Młody człowiek jest zazwyczaj pełen ciekawości życia.
– **Young men** are generally very curious about life.
(Note the plural form, to indicate generic meaning.)

3. Młody Prus był dzieckiem niesfornym i niefrasobliwym.
– **As a young** child, Prus was unruly and happy-go-lucky.

4. Mozart występował przed publicznością już w bardzo młodym wieku.
– **The young Mozart** gave public concerts at a very early age. It means 'Mozart when young gave public concerts'.

5. Taki młody chłopiec, a już w konflikcie z prawem!
– Such a **young boy**, and already in conflict with the law!
– A **mere youngster**, and already in conflict with the law!

6. Skąd młody Barker miał tyle pieniędzy, było zagadką dla wszystkich.
– Where **young Barker** had got so much money from, was a mystery to all.

7. Młoda para miała jechać do Paryża zaraz po ślubie.
– The **newly-weds** / The **young couple** / The **bride and bridegroom** were to leave for Paris immediately after the wedding.

8. Pan młody już czekał w kościele.
– The **bridegroom** was already waiting at the church.

9. Panna młoda miała na sobie przepiękną białą suknię.
– The **bride** was wearing a beautiful white wedding dress.

10. Młoda kadra zatrudniona w zeszłym tygodniu pracuje naprawdę świetnie.
– The **young staff** taken on last week are really coping very well.

11. Do kurczaka podano młode kartofle i marchewkę z groszkiem.
– **New** potatoes, and carrots and peas, were served with the chicken.

Młodzież

In Polish, 'młodzież' has a range of meanings, so in English diverse equivalents are used; the choice will depend on the context.

I. When it is clear that school pupils are meant, we can use **pupils** or **boys and girls**, e.g.

Na wycieczkę do Krakowa młodzież jechała autobusem szkolnym.
– On their outing to Cracow, the **pupils** went by school bus.

II. When 'młodzież' is a class noun, i.e. when it denotes a category of people, we may translate it as: a) **the young**, or b) **young people**, or c) **youngsters**.

Młodzież i jej problemy już od lat znajdują się w centrum naszych zainteresowań.

– For years our chief concern has been:
a) **the young** and their problems,
b) **young people** and their problems,
c) **youngsters** and their problems. *

But we can say:

Dzisiejsza młodzież czuje się zagubiona.
– **Youngsters** today feel lost.
– **The young** today feel lost.
– **Young people** today feel lost.

At a still higher level of abstraction, we can translate 'młodzież' as **youth** e.g.

Młodzież dziś czuje się zagubiona.
– **Youth** today feels lost.

Note that the definite article is not used, because here **youth** is generic, not specific. In this sentence we have no post-modification that would make **youth** specific. **The youth** with no post-modification would mean: 'młodzieniec' (**a young man**).

On the other hand, when **youth** is post-modified, therefore becoming specific (e.g. **the youth of Nazi Germany**), it is preceded by the definite article, e.g.

– The **youth** of today expect a lot.

But it is safer to avoid the word **youth** altogether, as its use is beset by pitfalls.

'Cała młodzież'
Say: **All young people** between the ages of 16 and 18.
Never say: the *whole youth*, or the *whole of the youth.*

III. When 'młodzież' is used to denote a specific group of young individuals, not a class noun, we can sometimes translate it as **the young people**, e.g.

* For a discussion of the definite article here, see: C. Kozłowska, *The Articles in English,* Ch. VI, 'All' and 'Class Nouns'.

Młodzież zgromadzona w sali powitała mówcę gorącymi oklaskami. – **The young people** in the hall applauded the speaker enthusiastically.

Note that the definite article is used here because **young people** is post-modified by the phrase *in the hall*, and therefore made specific.

More examples:
1. **The young** are not keen on listening to the old.
2. **School pupils**, especially High School pupils, protested strongly against having to wear the school badge on their coat.
3. He knew from experience how rapidly **young people's** moods change.
4. **Youngsters / young people / the young** get too much, and too little is expected of them.

More possible translations of 'młodzież':

1) **the students, the undergraduates**
2) **teenagers**
3) **the young**
4) **the younger generation** (note the comparative form: **younger**)
5) **young people**
6) **youngsters**

Cała młodzież Krakowa
WRONG – The whole youth of Cracow ...
RIGHT – All the **young people** of Cracow ...

Musieć

This is a word with which, when translating, Poles make many mistakes. This occurs mostly because 'musieć' has basically two meanings – one involving *inner compulsion*, and the other involving *external compulsion*. There are also difficulties with tenses; and sometimes other auxiliary verbs have to take the place of **must**.

I. *Affirmative*

Present tense

1. Muszę iść do lekarza.
– I **must** go to the doctor (*inner compulsion:* if I don't go, I won't get better).

2. Muszę iść do lekarza.
– I **have to** go to the doctor (Because he is expecting me. / I have an appointment with him. – *external compulsion*).

Future tense

3. Będę musiał iść do lekarza.
– I'**ll have to** go to the doctor (sometime, so that he can check my wound).

Note: 'musieć' has no future tense of its own.

Past tense

4. Musiałem to zrobić
– I **had to** do it (I had no other alternative – either *inner* or *external compulsion*).
– I **was forced / compelled** to do it (I was forced by someone to do it — *external compulsion*).

Must has no past tense of its own, and therefore one has to use synonyms, e.g. **to have to, be forced to, be compelled to**, e.g.
– **I was forced** by circumstances to cancel my appointment.
– I **had to** eat bread and water (for there was nothing else).

II. *Negative*

Present tense

Nie muszę tego zrobić.

RIGHT – I **don't have to** do it. / I **don't need to** do it.
WRONG – I mustn't do it. (This common mistake means: 'Nie wolno mi tego zrobić'.)

Nie muszę mu pomóc.
RIGHT – I **don't have to** help him. / I **don't need to** to help him.

WRONG – I mustn't help him.

Nie muszę iść do lekarza.

RIGHT – I **don't have to** go to the doctor. / I **don't need** to go to the doctor.

WRONG – I mustn't go to the doctor.

Past tense

Nie musiałem tego zrobić.

RIGHT – I **didn't have to** do it. / I **didn't need to do it**.

WRONG – I wasn't to do it.

Nie byłem zmuszony mu pomóc.

RIGHT – I **didn't have to** help him. / **I didn't need to help him.** / I wasn't **compelled** to help him.

WRONG – I hadn't to help him. / I **needn't** have helped him.

Future tense

Nie będę musiał tego zrobić.

RIGHT – I **shan't have to** do it. / I **won't need to** do it.

(Use the verb **need**.)

Nauka

One would seem justified in asserting that many mistakes are made by Poles when translating 'nauka' or 'naukowy', for they often translate these words as **scientific**, and as **science**.

In English, science means **pure science** or one of the pure sciences (exact sciences, such as physics, biology, astronomy, etc.) in which measurement is possible. The Polish language, on the other hand, assigns a broader meaning to 'nauka', 'naukowiec' and 'naukowy', which do not necessarily include quantitative measurements. 'Nauka' may mean **scholarship** in general, i.e. acquisition of knowledge, academic, theoretical thinking, (body of) learning, knowledge, research work; also: study, studies, schooling, or education.

In Polish, the plural form of 'nauka' is often used – e.g. 'nauki ścisłe' etc., whereas the singular is more common in English, e.g. **pure science, applied science, medical science, the science of acoustics**. The English word **learning** is not generally used with regard to study, or to the acquisition of scientific knowledge.

One instance of the misuse of **science** to signify 'nauka' is seen in the name of the well-known publishing house 'Wydawnictwo Naukowe PWN', normally translated as **Polish Scientific Publishers**. This title would suggest that the firm publishes works dealing exclusively with pure, abstract, exact science, which is not the case. A better, less misleading name would be **Polish Academic Publishers**.

Niedawno, dopiero niedawno, od niedawna

We may take these three phrases in turn. They are all similar, but differ in where the emphasis falls, and this is linked with their position in the sentence.

Some sentences to illustrate this are given below.

I. *'Niedawno' (referring to a point of time):*

Widziałem go niedawno.
– I saw him **quite recently**.
– I saw him **not long ago**.

Niedawno zacząłem uczyć się angielskiego.
– I've **recently** begun to learn English. (The stress is on *learning English.*)
– I began to learn English **not long ago**. (emphasis on *when*)

Widziałem go w teatrze niedawno.
– I saw him in the theatre **recently**. (emphasis on *time*)
– I saw him in the theatre **not long ago**, (emphasis on *time*)
– I saw him **recently** in the theatre. (emphasis on *place*)
– I saw him **not long ago** in the theatre, (emphasis on *place*)
– **Not long ago** I saw him in the theatre. (emphasis on *place*)

II. *'Dopiero niedawno'*

Wilson dopiero niedawno odkrył Waugha.
– Wilson (had) **only recently** discovered Waugh.

Dopiero niedawno kupiliśmy nowy dom.
– **Just recently** we bought a new house.

III. *'Od niedawna'*

Od niedawna chodzę na koncerty.
– **Recently** I've started going to concerts. (emphasis on *going to concerts*)

Chodzę na koncerty od niedawna.
– I've **only recently** started going to concerts. (emphasis on *recently*)

Od niedawna mam samochód.
– I've **recently** acquired a car. (emphasis on *acquired a car*)

Mam samochód od niedawna.
– I have**n't** had a car **for very** long. (emphasis on *time*)
– I acquired a car **not long ago**. (emphasis on *acquisition of car*)

Znam go od niedawna.
– I have**n't** known him **for very long**. (Note the use of the negative.)
– I first met him **not long ago**. (emphasis on *time*)

Niedawno spotkałem go na ulicy.
– A short **while ago** I met him in the street. (emphasis on *meeting*)

Useful phrases of time:

a short time ago, not long ago, the other day, recently, a few days ago, lately, a short while ago

Obiekt

Stanisławski's *The Great Polish-English Dictionary* gives four meanings of the Polish word 'obiekt': 1) przedmiot–**object**, 2) przedmiot poznania–**subject**, 3) cel–**target**; **objective**, 4) budynek – **building**, **structure**.

Here we shall deal only with this last, fourth meaning. Remember that in translating the first three meanings of ‘obiekt’ given by Stanisławski, we can use the English word **object**, as in the following examples: object of *interest* (here ‘object’ means **target**), object of *attention*, object of *desire*, object of *hate*, object of *love*, object of *affection* (abstracts).

But the English word **object** cannot be used with reference to a building, etc., for in that concrete sense **object** means **thing** (przedmiot) (e.g. There was a large **object** lying on the table).

In this meaning, it is wrong to translate the Polish ‘obiekt’ by the English word **object**.

When ‘obiekt’ is unaccompanied by a qualifier such as ‘przemysłowy’, ‘historyczny’ etc., we should simply translate it as **building** (or as **structure** if a bridge, etc. is meant), e.g.

Obiekty te, pilnie strzeżone, należą do marynarki wojennej.
– These **buildings**, which are heavily guarded, belong to the navy.

Oba te obiekty projektował Tylman van Gameren.
– Both **buildings** were designed by Tylman van Gameren.

Now let us take some examples where ‘obiekt’ is post-modified by an adjective or adjectival phrase, e.g.

a) ‘obiekt przemysłowy’ – **industrial works** (always plural), or **industrial plant**

W latach siedemdziesiątych wybudowano wiele ważnych obiektów przemysłowych.
– A lot of important **industrial works** were built in the seventies.

b) ‘obiekt historyczny’ – **historical building**

W Warszawie znajduje się wiele obiektów historycznych.
– There are many **historical buildings** in Warsaw.

c) ‘obiekt architektury sakralnej’ – **sacred building, example of ecclesiastical architecture**

Katedra Wawelska jest najsłynniejszym obiektem architektury sakralnej w Polsce.
– Wawel Cathedral is the most famous **sacred building** in Poland.

d) ‘obiekty cywilne’ – **municipal buildings**

Prawie wszystkie obiekty cywilne w stolicy ucierpiały od ataków bombowych.
– Nearly all the **municipal buildings** in the capital were damaged by bombing.

e) ‘obiekty użyteczności publicznej’ – **public utilities**

‘Obiekt’ — extra sentences:

Wydział Urbanistyki zajmuje się projektowaniem i budową różnych obiektów użyteczności publicznej.
– The Department of Town Planning deals with the design and construction of various **public utilities**.

Członkowie bandy prawdopodobnie przechowują u siebie około 10 obiektów sakralnych z 20 zrabowanych tuż przed Bożym Narodzeniem.
– Members of the gang are probably still hiding about ten of the twenty **sacred works of art** stolen just before Christmas.

Mimo iż uznano już dawno, że muzeum w Pszczynie jest słabo chronione, przekazano pieniądze na założenie elektronicznego systemu ochrony dopiero dzień po okradzeniu tego obiektu.
– Although it was realised long since that the Pszczyna Museum was poorly protected, it was not until the **museum** was robbed that money was provided for the installation of an electronic alarm system.

Od ... do; od ... po

Note the following sentences, paying attention to the case endings:

1. Od pierwszego momentu do ostatniej chwili naszej znajomości miałem wrażenie, że on kłamie.
– **From the first to the very last moment** of our acquaintance I felt that he was lying.

2. Od połowy września do końca roku trwały poszukiwania.
– **From** the middle of September **till** (not: **to**) the end of the year the search continued.

'od ... po'

3. Od Malibu Beach po Palm Springs oferuje amerykański żigolak atrakcyjnym, bogatym damom miłość i seks.
– **From** Malibu Beach **to / as far as** Palm Springs the American gigolo offers attractive, rich women love and sex.

Osoby

Note that in English the plural of **person** is not **persons**, but **people**, e.g.

Było tylko pięć osób w pokoju.
– There were only **five people** in the room.

z Pietyzmem

Here are some words and phrases which may come in useful when translating texts connected with the repair and restoration of war-damaged buildings, etc.

NOUNS:

the national heritage, monuments, historical buildings, famous monuments and buildings

VERBS:

cherish, revere, reconstruct, restore, look after

ADJECTIVES:

old, famous, historical, badly damaged, bombed, bombarded, devastated during the war, reduced to rubble, set on fire

ADVERBS:

carefully, devotedly, lovingly, patiently, piously, solicitously, with great care, with the greatest of care, with loving care

Sentences:

1. Do końca życia przechowywała z największym pietyzmem pamiątki po bracie.
– To the end of her life she **deeply** cherished her surviving mementos of her brother.

2. Cały naród patrzy na dziedzictwo narodowe z największym pietyzmem.
– The whole nation looks upon the national heritage as something **to be revered and cherished**.

3. Po wojnie ludność Warszawy odbudowała z pietyzmem zniszczoną historyczną część stolicy.
– After the war, the people of Warsaw rebuilt the devastated historical part of the capital **with meticulous care / attention to detail**.

Po ... (referring to time)

When 'po' refers to past time, it can be translated by **after**, or **later**, or **past**, or **afterwards**, but these words are not interchangeable, as we shall see below.

Note that **after** and **past** *precede* the noun, whereas **later** and **afterwards** *come after* the noun.

Here are some examples.

A.

1) Use **after** to translate 'po' preceding a noun of time, when that noun indicates a point of time, e.g.

Włamanie do domu zdarzyło się tuż po północy.
– The break-in took place just **after** midnight. (point of time)

2) Use **later**, following the relevant noun, when the noun denotes not a point of time, but a period (continuum of time), e.g.

Chociaż spotkali się znowu po roku, Marysia ledwo poznała swojego brata.
– Although they met a year **later** (period of time), Mary scarcely recognised her brother.

Similarly:

Widziała brata w czerwcu, a jego zgon nastąpił po miesiącu.
– She saw her brother in June, and he died a month **later**. (N.B. not '**After** a month', but meaning 'at the **end** of a month' – at the end of a specific period of time.)

3) Use either **after** or **past** with a specific point of time, e.g.

Wrócił do domu po dwunastej w nocy.
– It was **after midnight** when he came home.

One might equally well say:

– It was **past midnight** when he came home.

These two versions are almost, but not entirely identical in meaning, for **after midnight** seems rather to be neutral in tone, while **past midnight** appears to contain a note of disapproval.

4) Instead of translating 'po wielu latach' as **after many years**, we can say **many years later**, or **many years afterwards**.

Similarly, instead of translating 'po chwili' as **after a short while**, we can say **a short while afterwards**. And we can translate 'po dłuższym czasie' as **a long time afterwards** or **after a long time**, but not **a long time later**.

With **years**:

CORRECT – **after** many years / many years **later** / many years **afterwards**
CORRECT – **after** a long time / a long time **afterwards / much later**
WRONG – a long time later

B. *Here 'po' indicates the end of some activity – looking to the future.* Note the following sentences:

Po szkole Piotr chciałby dostać się na uniwersytet.
– **After** school Peter would like to go to university.

Po zakończeniu szkoły chciałby studiować medycynę.
– **After** finishing school he would like to go in for medicine.

C. *Case ending of the noun after 'po':*

In the following examples, note the case-ending of the nouns following 'po':

po północy (locative case) – **after** midnight
po roku (locative case) – **after** a year
po miesiącu (locative case) – **after** a month, etc.

But if a noun ends not in the locative case, as above, but in the accusative, the meaning of 'po' is not **after**, but **till, up to**, etc., e.g.

po dzień dzisiejszy – **till today**, **up till today**, **up to this very day**, e.g.

Zapłaciłem czynsz po dzień dzisiejszy.
– I've paid the rent **up till** today.

Once again, it is advisable to use **after** when it precedes a noun meaning a point in time e.g.

– It happened **after** midnight.

Use **later** *following* a noun that denotes not a point of time, but a stretch of time, e.g.

– It happened a month **later**. (i.e. at the end of a month, after a month had elapsed).

Po wielu latach – **after** many years (many years **later**)
Po chwili – **after** a short while (a short while afterwards)
Po dłuższym czasie – **after** a long time (not: 'a long time later', but a '**long time afterwards**')

'Po' – extra sentences:

1. Po dniu dzisiejszym dni będą dłuższe.
– **After** today, the days will be longer.

2. Po 20 latach nieobecności absolutnie nie mógł poznać swego miasta.
– **After** twenty years' absence, he was completely unable to recognise his home town.

3. Po 25. każdego miesiąca nie mam już pieniędzy.
– I never have any money **after** the 25th of the month.

4. Skończę to tłumaczenie po 20 grudnia.
– I'll finish my translation **after** the 20th of December.

If the Polish text were: 'Do 20 grudnia'; this would be in English:
– I'll finish my translation **by / before** the 20th of December.

Podczas gdy ...

This Polish phrase can be used in either of two situations.

One of the following sentences points to simultaneity of two situations, while the other indicates opposition:

1) *Same time:*

Podczas gdy Marcin pracował w Gdyni, jego brat Bronek studiował w Krakowie.
– **While** Marcin was working in Gdynia, his brother Bronek was studying in Cracow.

2) *Contrast (opposition):*

Podczas gdy Zygmunt Freud był lekarzem psychiatrą, jego wnuk, Lucien Freud, jest znanym malarzem portrecistą.
– **Whereas** Sigmund Freud was a doctor and psychoanalyst, his grandson, Lucien Freud, is an eminent portrait painter.

Podobnie jak ...

Compare the following two groups of sentences:

I. In this group, attention is drawn to **similarity** between people. In these sentences, 'podobnie jak' connects nouns, or nouns with pronouns, e.g.

1. Dziewczynki, podobnie jak chłopcy, nie lubią chodzić do szkoły.
– Girls, **like** boys, don't like going to school.

2. Jego ojciec, podobnie jak on, jest lekarzem.
– His father, **like** him, is a doctor.

3. Podobnie jak Jan, nie mam zdania w tej sprawie.
– **Like** John, I've no opinion on the matter.

4. Robert będzie studiował na wydziale biologii, podobnie jak ja.
– Robert is going to study biology, **like** me.

Thus here we have people compared:
Dziewczynki ... podobnie jak chłopcy – like boys
Jego ojciec ... podobnie jak on – **like** him
Ja ... podobnie jak Jan – **like** John
Robert ... podobnie jak ja – **like** me

Rule. In comparison involving people, use **like**, never **as**.
Note that in English if a pronoun follows **like**, it is in the accusative case (biernik): (like **him**, like **me**), etc.

II. In this group, emphasis is not so much on the kind of people concerned, as on the way they behave, so emphasis is on the verb:

5. Connors zachowuje się podobnie jak McEnroe.
– Connors **behaves** the **same way as** McEnroe.
(In English, the connecting word is **as**).

6. Andrzej myśli podobnie jak Krzysztof.
– Andrew thinks the same way **as** Christopher.
– Andrew thinks the same **as** Christopher (**does**).

General rule: In such sentences, before a noun or a pronoun use **like** (**like** our teacher, **like** her); with verb, use **as**: (**as** they do, **as** he behaves, **as** Christopher thinks, etc).

III. Here is a sentence which we shall use as an illustration of right and wrong usage of **like** and **as**:

7. Podobnie jak jego ojciec, Jerzy chciał zostać inżynierem.
George wanted to be an engineer, **like** his father.

WRONG – similar to... / just as his brother... / analogously to his father / as Robert

RIGHT – **like** his father / **like** his brother / **like** his father / **like** Robert

WRONG and RIGHT

1. Podobnie jak ojciec, jego stryj także jest prawnikiem.
WRONG – His uncle, the same as his father, is a lawyer.
RIGHT – **Like** his father, his uncle, too, is a lawyer.

2. Podobnie jak w języku polskim, w rosyjskim nie ma rodzajników.
WRONG – Like in Polish, there are no articles in Russian, either.
RIGHT – **Like** Polish, Russian has no articles either.
RIGHT – **As** in Polish, there are no articles in Russian, either.

3. Podobnie jak i ja, Ryszard ożenił się bardzo młodo.
WRONG – Just the same as I, Richard got married very young.
RIGHT – **Like me**, Richard got married very young.

4. Podobnie jak Jan, nie mam zdania w tej sprawie.
WRONG – Just as John, I have no opinion on the matter.
RIGHT – **Like** John, I have no opinion on the matter.

5. Obserwuj go, i zrób podobnie jak on.
WRONG – Observe him, and do similarly to him.
RIGHT – Watch him, and **do** (the same) **as he does**.

6. Jestem ubrany podobnie jak wczoraj.
WRONG – I'm dressed similar to yesterday.
RIGHT – I'm dressed **the same way** as I was yesterday.
I'm dressed **as** I was yesterday.

7. Podobnie jak w ubiegłym roku, tego lata znowu pojedziemy w góry.

WRONG – Same way as last year, this summer, too, we'll be going to the mountains.

RIGHT – This summer we'll be going to the mountains again, (the) same **as** last year.

Podstawa

Base and **basis** are the closest and most commom equivalents used for translating 'podstawa'. But quite often the translator is not sure which of these two English terms to use. Some rough guidance may be sought by applying the English term **base** to cases where the Polish word 'podstawa' refers to something concrete, something which has physical existence, e.g. we say 'the **base** of a statue' (meaning the lower part on which the main part – figure, etc. rests). We also say **naval base** (to which ships return), **base camp**, etc. – in other words, something concrete.

But this concrete meaning (as something on which other things rest, as constituting a support), has been co-opted into the more abstract part of the language, and can be applied to abstracts, in which case we use **basis**.

1. Mogę powiedzieć na podstawie moich doświadczeń, że wasz plan się nie uda.
– I may as well say, on the **basis** of my own experience, that your plan will not succeed.

2. Niestety podstawa tej figurki jest pęknięta.
– Unfortunately the **base** of that statuette is cracked.

3. Moja praca w szkole w charakterze nauczycielki jest podstawą mego bytu.
– My job as a school teacher constitutes the **basis** of my existence.

Apart from **base** and **basis**, several other words can be used as equivalents of 'podstawa', e.g. **foundation**, or **grounds**.

4. Łacina stwarza doskonałą podstawę dla nauki języków nowożytnych.
– Latin constitutes an excellent **foundation** for learning modern languages.
5. Nie masz absolutnie żadnych podstaw, aby tak twierdzić.
– You have absolutely no **grounds** for saying that.
6. Chciałbym nauczyć się języka chińskiego, ale musiałbym zacząć od podstaw.
– I would like to learn Chinese, but I would have to start **from the very beginning**.
7. Nie ma realnych podstaw, aby podejrzewać tego człowieka.
– There's no **real reason** for suspecting the man.

Pomijając coś

This can be translated in a number of ways. In some cases, the equivalent of 'pomijając coś' comes at the beginning of the sentence, and in other cases at the end.

As equivalents of 'pomijając coś' we find: 1) **apart from** + noun, 2) noun + **aside**, 3) **in addition to** + noun, 4) **not to mention..**. sth, 5) **disregarding** sth, 6) **if we ignore** sth, 7) **despite** sth ..., 8) **to say nothing** of sth ...

'Pomijając' may have either of two meanings: a) **in addition to**, or b) **passing over** sth ...
Here are some examples:

'Pomijając' sth, positive:

1. Pomijając jego zasługi wojenne (sth positive), miał za sobą wspaniałą karierę naukową.
– **Apart from** his fine war record, / **In addition to** his fine war record, he had a splendid academic career.
2. Pomijając zalety stylu (sth positive), książka ta jest doskonałym świadectwem tego okresu.
– **In addition to** its impressive style / **Virtues of** style **aside** / / **Without even mentioning** its fine style the book provides a fine record of the period.

'Pomijając' sth, negative:

1. Pomijając ogromne korzyści, które mogłyby z tego planu wyniknąć, można by się również spodziewać wielkich strat.
   – **Despite** the tremendous advantages to be had from the scheme, no doubt serious losses could ensue as well.
2. Sprawozdawca ograniczył się do podania wyniku spotkania, pomijając milczeniem przykry incydent zaistniały w drugiej połowie meczu.
   – The commentator confined himself to giving the result of the match, **making no mention of** the unpleasant incident which occurred in the second half of the game.
3. Pomijając jego młody wiek, kandydat niewątpliwie był za mało zdolny i za mało doświadczony, aby objąć to stanowisko.
   – **In addition to / Apart from** his lack of years, the applicant was really not talented enough or experienced enough for the job.

Porównanie (W porównaniu z czymś)

Instead of translating this as **in comparison with**, we can simplify matters by using a construction with **than**, e.g.

Produkcja całego przemysłu zwiększyła się w porównaniu z rokiem 1938 prawie 9 razy.
– Total industrial output was nearly 9 times greater **than** in 1938.

Pozytywny

Although there is an English word, **positive**, very similar in appearance to the Polish word 'pozytywny', the meanings of these two words are often quite different.

Positive in English means **sure, certain**, **definite**, **explicit**, whereas the Polish word 'pozytywny' means **good** (e.g. 'pozytywny człowiek' – it is equal to the slang epithet **a good guy**); it also means, not with regard to people but to actions, moves, etc. **affirmative, favourable, advantageous, salutary**, **friendly**, **successful**, **desired**, **beneficial**, **useful**, **conciliatory**, **satisfactory**, **constructive**.

Nearly every sentence containing the word 'pozytywny' has to be translated into English idiomatically. Two sentences are given here to illustrate this point:

1. Leczenie to nie daje pozytywnych wyników.
– The treatment is not producing **the desired effect**.

An idiomatic translation would be even better:

– The treatment **isn't working**.

2. Edward oczekuje pozytywnego wyniku egzaminu.
– Edward expects a **pass** in his exam.

An idiomatic translation would be even better:

– Edward expects to **pass** his exam.

Better still (informal):

Edward expects to **get through** his exam.

The translation of 'pozytywny' itself will depend on which English noun it qualifies, for the Polish noun qualified by 'pozytywny' may have diverse equivalents in English, and if so, the translation will depend not on the Polish but on the English noun used. This is illustrated by the first two sentences given above, where 'pozytywny wynik egzaminu' could be translated as **pass in an exam**, while 'pozytywny wynik leczenia' could be translated in terms of **successful effect of treatment**. 'Wynik' is the Polish word used in both examples, but by itself gives us too little information on which to base an adequate translation. We must know 'wynik czego' (the result of **what**?). Thus 'wynik egzaminu' will be **mark in an exam**, while 'wynik leczenia' will be **effect of treatment**. In the end we arrive at **pass** and **successful / desired effect**. In a few cases, however, we can translate 'pozytywny' as **positive**, e.g.

pozytywny odzew na apel
– a **positive** response to an appeal,

pozytywne nastawienie do pracy
– a **positive** attitude to work (a willingness to work).

But mostly we translate 'pozytywny' with the help of quite a wide range of English adjectives. A selection of these is given below:

otrzymać pozytywną ocenę planu – get a plan **approved**; get **approval** for a plan

przedstawić coś w pozytywnym świetle – show sth in a **good** light

pozytywna próba (maszyny, itd.) – **successful test / trial**

pozytywny wynik egzaminu – **pass mark** in an exam

pozytywny wynik rozmów – **successful outcome** of talks

pozytywny wynik leczenia – **successful effect** of treatment

pozytywny efekt kary – **salutary effect** of punishment

pozytywne działanie kremu na cerę – **beneficial good effect** of cream on the skin

pozytywny efekt zmiany klimatu na zdrowie – **beneficial effect** of a change of climate on sb's health

pozytywny obrót wydarzeń – **turn for the better**

otrzymać pozytywną odpowiedź na list – receive **an affirmative** reply to a letter

otrzymać pozytywną odpowiedź na podanie – receive word that one's application has been **granted**

zgodzić się na pozytywne załatwienie sprawy – agree to settle a matter **to sb's satisfaction**

pozytywna prognoza – **bright, optimistic, propitious** outlook / forecast

pozytywne nastawienie do pracy / do ludzi / do świata – **go-ahead, energetic attitude to work / friendly attitude** to people/**friendly, outgoing, cheerful attitude** to the world

pozytywne nastawienie do problemu – **constructive / reasonable** approach to the problem

English headwords:

Here are some English words and phrases often collocated with 'pozytywny' which might be useful:

1) positive (the opposite of *negative* result of a test for cancer; he test turned out to be **positive**, (i, e. cancer was present)

2) *answer (settle) / grant* sth

obtain a **reply in the affirmative**

receive word that an **application** has been **granted**

accede to a **request**

settle sth **to sb's satisfaction**
be obliged for a **favourable reply**
look for a **positive response**
3) *terms* of an *offer* (= warunki)
obtain **good / advantageous / favourable terms**
4) *succeed*
pass a certain **standard** (the opposite of *fail*)
get a **pass mark**
pass a **test**
have a **successful outcome / test / trial**
obtain **approval** for sth
5) *effect*
have an **advantageous / beneficial / desired / good / salutary / useful** effect (each of these adjectives collocates with different nouns)
6) *outlook* (chances for the future)
promising / propitious outlook
7) *attitude, feelings*
positive: = vigorous / energetic / enthusiastic / attitude to work; **friendly** attitude to people; **friendly / outgoing / cheerful** attitude to the world; **positive: = energetic** approach to a problem or sphere of action; **constructive / reasonable** approach to a problem
8) *moral character*
good man; admirable / estimable / praiseworthy character; man **to be admired, good guy** (slang) (in a film, etc.)

Problem

The Polish word 'problem' can be translated into English as **problem, matter, difficulty, question, issue, item**. These words are more or less interchangeable. Here are some examples:

1. AIDS jest wciąż nie rozwiązanym problemem.
Aids is still an **unsolved problem**.

2. Podstawowym problemem staje się transport gotowych towarów.
– Our basic **difficulty** is to find out how to transport the final product.

3. Problem poruszony przez mówcę jest o tyle ciekawy, iż rzeczywiście w literaturze młodzieżowej uczyniono z Sitting Bulla wielkiego indiańskiego herosa.
– The **question** mentioned by the speaker is an interesting one, in that books for teenagers do indeed present Sitting Bull as a great Red Indian hero.

4. Kwestia transportu jest naszym największym problemem.
– Our greatest **problem** is that of transport.

5. Na konferencji poruszono wiele problemów o międzynarodowym znaczeniu.
– Many **issues** of international importance were raised at the conference.

6. Dowóz czarnych niewolników stał się problemem absolutnie pierwszorzędnej wagi dla nowych panów Ameryki.
– Supplies of black slaves became a **matter** of crucial importance to the new masters of America.

7. To było ich największym problemem.
– That was their greatest **difficulty**.

8. Pozostał nam tylko jeden problem do omówienia.
– There's only one more **item on the agenda** to be dealt with.

Procent

Miasto w 85% zniszczone.
– A city 85 per cent destroyed.
– A city which was 85 per cent destroyed.
– A city 85 per cent of which was destroyed.

Program TV

Whereas Polish people speak of 'Program pierwszy TV", 'Program drugi', etc., native English speakers say: **Channel One, Channel Two**, etc.

na Przełomie

The most usual way to translate 'na przełomie' when two numbers are involved is to translate the second number, and ignore the first, e.g.

1) *Centuries:*

na przełomie XIV i XV wieku
– **at the turn of** the 15th century

Note: Roman numerals are used to denote the centuries in Polish, but Arabic ones in English.

2) *Decades:*

na przełomie lat dwudziestych i trzydziestych
– at the end of the twenties and the beginning of the thirties

3) *Months:*

na przełomie maja i czerwca
– **at the end of** May and the beginning of June
– **as** May **passed into** June

4) *Periods of history:*

na przełomie wieków średnich i Odrodzenia
– during the **transitional period** from the Middle Ages to the Renaissance
na przełomie feudalizmu i kapitalizmu
– **during the transition** from feudalism to capitalism

5) *Days:*

w nocy z 7-ego na 8-ego maja
– **during the night** of May 7th

6) *Geological eras:*

na przełomie triasu i jury
– **as** the Triassic **was succeeded** by the Jurassic

7) *Sources of energy:*

na przełomie epoki wytwarzania energii z węgla i energii nuklearnej
– **as** coal-based energy production **gives way to** nuclear energy

Przestrzegać czegoś

Affirmative

Our translation of 'przestrzegać czegoś" will depend on the direct object of the verb.

Note that in Polish the noun used in the function of the direct object here appears, not in the accusative case (biernik), but in the genitive (dopełniacz). Here are some examples:

przestrzegać diety – **keep to / stick** to / **watch** one's diet
przestrzegać dyscypliny – **keep / maintain** discipline
przestrzegać etykiety – **keep to / observe** the rules of etiquette
przestrzegać form towarzyskich – **keep to** the polite conventions
przestrzegać higieny – **be particular about** cleanliness
przestrzegać nakazów naszego sumienia – **act according** to our conscience / **obey** our conscience / **follow** the dictates of our conscience
przestrzegać porządku publicznego – **preserve** law and order
przestrzegać prawa – **abide by / obey / keep within / respect / stick to** the law
przestrzegać przepisów drogowych – **obey** the Highway Code
przestrzegać przepisów prawa – **keep within** the law
przestrzegać litery prawa – **adhere to / keep to** the letter of the law.

Thus in the *affirmative* we have: 'przestrzegać przepisów' – **abide by / act according to / adhere to / comply with / conform to / follow / / obey / observe / stick to** (most informal) the rules and regulations, etc.

Negative

In the *negative* we have: 'nie przestrzegać przepisów' – **disregard / disobey / fail to observe / flout / ignore / infringe / violate** the rules, etc.

1. Nieprzestrzeganie przepisów BHP grozi karą 10 lat więzienia.
– **Infringement** of the Safety Regulations carries a penalty of ten years in prison.

2. Nigdy nie przestrzegając przepisów, pan ST nie wyróżniał się wśród otoczenia.
– In constantly **disregarding the rules**, Mr ST was no different from anybody else.

3. Kierowcę obowiązuje ścisłe przestrzeganie przepisów drogowych.
– Drivers are required to comply with the Highway Code at all times.

4. Nieprzestrzeganie przepisów było przyczyną wypadku.
– The accident was caused by **failure to obey the regulations.**

Reklama (TV)

In Britain people often use the word **commercials**.

Reprezentacyjny

This is a word which is fairly commonly used in Polish. But it never means **representative** in English.

The Polish word 'reprezentacyjny' generally means **grand, imposing**, as in the following examples:

1. Teraz wchodzimy do mniej reprezentacyjnej części tej budowli.
– We come now to the **less grand** parts of the building.

2. W czasie pobytu królowej apartamenty reprezentacyjne są niedostępne dla publiczności.
– While the Queen is in residence, the **State Rooms / State Apartments** are closed to the public.

Used in connection with a woman, 'reprezentacyjny' means **attractive, smart, elegant, distinguished in appearance, dress and manner**, e.g.

3. Ze względu na karierę chciał ożenić się z kobietą reprezentacyjną.
– Because of his career, he was anxious to marry a **distinguished / / elegant / smart / striking-looking** woman / a woman **who would be an asset to him**.

4. Jego stanowisko wymaga, aby mieszkali w dzielnicy reprezentacyjnej.

– His job obliges them to live in **one of the best districts / in a smart / fashionable / an exclusive district**.

5. Kompania reprezentacyjna położyła wieniec na grobie.
– **The Guard of Honour** laid a wreath at the tomb.

6. Łazienki (park i pałac) spełniają też funkcje reprezentacyjne – oficjalnych gości też trzeba gdzieś przyjąć.
– The Łazienki Palace also acts as a **show-piece**, as official visitors need to be entertained somwhere.

Rodzaj (w rodzaju czegoś)

Note the following translations:

1. Czy on rzeczywiście powiedział coś w tym rodzaju?
– Did he really say **something like that? / of that sort? / of that kind?**

2. Przy ścianie stało coś w rodzaju szafy.
– Against the wall there was **a kind of** cupboard. / a **sort of** cupboard.

3. Kiedy szłam przez las, słyszałam coś jakby wołanie o pomoc.
– As I was walking through the woods, I heard **something like** a cry for help / something that **sounded like** a cry for help.

4. Przewodniczący ciągle robił uwagi w rodzaju: 'Opowiada pan bzdury'.
– The chairman kept coming out with **such** remarks **as:** 'You're talking absolute rubbish'.

5. W najniższym grobie neolitowym były narzędzia w rodzaju kilofów.
– In the lowest of these graves there were tools **such as** picks.

6. Suknia jej była zrobiona z materiału w rodzaju jedwabiu.
– Her dress was made of a **silky** material.

Compare: **silk** (noun) – **silky** (adjective)
poplin (noun) – **popliny** (adjective)
wool (noun) – **woolly** (adjective)

8. Pomijając fakt, że tego rodzaju wnioski są całkowicie nielogiczne, moralne implikacje byłyby katastrofalne.
– Apart from the fact that the conclusions **he came to** are completely illogical, the moral implications would be disastrous.

Rozkwit

The Polish word 'rozkwit', the second syllable of which is connected with the Polish noun for **flower** ('kwiat'), or with the verb **bloom** ('kwitnąć'), lends itself to translation by means of metaphors that include floral associations, such as: **be in full flower, burgeon, reach full bloom, reach its fullest / greatest flowering, its greatest efflorescence**, etc. These are particularly suitable metaphors to use in connection with the arts, and especially with painting. Some examples are given below.

Culture generally

1. Kultura polska osiągnęła swój największy rozkwit w XVIII wieku.
– The greatest **efflorescence** of Polish culture took place in the 18th century.
– Polish culture enjoyed its **golden age** in the eighteenth century.
– Polish culture reached its **apogee** in the eighteenth century.

2. Wielki rozkwit talentów Prousta, Valéry'ego i Gide'a po 1914 ...
– The great, post-1914 **flowering** of the tálents of Proust, Valéry and Gide ...

3. Pełen rozkwit romantyzmu nastąpił w Polsce w pierwszej połowie XIX wieku.
– The **blossoming / burgeoning** of Romanticism in Poland reached its **peak** in the first half of the nineteenth century.
– The first half of the nineteenth century saw the full **flowering** of the Romantic movement in Poland.

Music

4. W muzyce okres Odrodzenia odznaczał się bujnym rozkwitem wielogłosowości.
– In the sphere of music, the Renaissance was marked by a rich **burgeoning** of polyphony.

Literature

5. W XVI w. nastąpił rozkwit liryki (Ronsard).
– In the sixteenth century, the lyric poets, such as Ronsard, **came very much to the fore**.

Town planning

6. W tym okresie nastąpił rozkwit urbanistyczny.
– At that time **tremendous changes** took place in the area of town planning.

Painting

7. Rozkwit malarstwa renesansowego we Włoszech przypadł na wiek XV.
– Italian Renaissance painting reached its **apogee** in the fifteenth century.

8. Największy rozkwit malarstwa holenderskiego nastąpił w XVII wieku.
– Dutch painting reached its fullest **splendour** / was at its **most brilliant** / reached **its peak** in the seventeenth century.

Sculpture

9. W XV wieku nastąpił rozkwit rzeźby gotyckiej.
– The fifteenth century saw the **emergence** and **growing popularity** of Gothic sculpture in the round.

Nauka

10. O rozkwicie nauki w czasie Odrodzenia zdecydowały przeważnie kierunki empiryczne i eksperymentalne.
– **Advances** in scholarship and learning during the Renaissance were chiefly rooted in the experimental, empirical disciplines.

The humanities

11. Odrodzenie było okresem wielkiego rozkwitu nauk humanistycznych.
– The Renaissance was the **golden age** of the humanities.

But the word 'rozkwit' is not necessarily confined to such spheres as art, painting, etc., to which the flower motif is appropriate. One can also apply the word 'rozkwit' to more concrete things, such as a great empire, a town or city, or even a religion, e.g.

12. W okresie swego największego rozkwitu Rzym panował nad całym prawie światem.
– At the **height / peak of its power,** the Roman Empire ruled over nearly all of the then-known world.

As usual, the translation of 'rozkwit' depends on the noun collocating with it.

Thus if the Polish word 'rozkwit' occurs in a context referring to an **empire**, a **city, town**, etc., we can translate the phrase containing 'rozkwit' as:

- attained **its greatest glory**
- reached the **apex** of its power and influence
- reached the **zenith** of its power.

As far as empires and countries are concerned, we can often use the word **rise** to denote 'rozkwit', e.g.

13. Rozkwit Chin do rangi potęgi światowej odczuwano jako zagrożenie dla Zachodu.
– The **rise** of China to world-power status was seen as a threat to the western world.

In another context, we find the phrase **prime of life** denoting a person's best period, e.g.

14. Poeta zmarł w rozkwicie życia, mając zaledwie 35 lat.
– The poet died in **the prime of life,** at the age of only 35.

15. Kiedy malowano ten jej portret, była w pełnym rozkwicie swej młodości i urody.
– When her portraits were painted, she was in the full flush of youth and beauty.

Extra sentences for practice

16. Kościół ten został zbudowany w okresie rozkwitu baroku.
– The church was built at the **height of** the baroque.

17. Katedra w Chartres reprezentuje rozkwit architektury gotyckiej.
– Chartres Cathedral represents the **acme** of Gothic architecture.

18. Po największym rozkwicie klasycyzmu, nastąpił zwrot w kierunku romantyzmu.
– The **flowering** of classicism was followed by a shift towards Romanticism.

19. Rozkwit rock and rolla nastąpił w latach 1960/61.
– Rock and roll had its **heyday** during 1960–61.

20. Rozkwit rosyjskiego baletu oszałamiał cały świat.
– The **splendour / brilliance** of the Russian ballet dazzled the whole world.

Rzadziej

One can translate 'rzadziej' as **less often, less frequently**, **not so often**, rather than **more seldom**.

Skarb

The Polish word 'skarb' has many different equivalents, such as those given below:

a) 'skarb' (sing.) – **treasure, hoard** (collection of objects hidden or found, objects stored away in secret), 'skarby' (pl) – **valuable artefacts** (collected); **valuables**; **hoard**; **treasure-trove** (valuable things once hidden, later rediscovered); **treasures** (things loved and collected);

b) 'skarb'– a place where valuables are held, e.g. Skarb Państwa – **Exchequer**;

c) 'skarb' – an abstract **valuable** (e.g. asset);

d) sometimes the word 'skarb' is applied when referring to a loved, admired, cherished person. Its equivalent in English could be: **darling, dear, deary** (colloq., half-joking), **sweetie, treasure** (informal, half-joking), **sweetheart** (informal).

Some illustrative sentences are given below:

1. Dziś nikt już nie szuka ukrytych **skarbów** z nadzieją na szybkie wzbogacenie się.
– Nobody nowadays looks for **treasure-troves** in the hope of getting rich quick.
(*See* a.)

2. Gdyby ktoś znalazł w ziemi skarb w postaci złotych monet, musiałby oddać je do Skarbu Państwa.
– If somebody happened to find a hoard of gold coins hidden in the ground, they would have to hand them over to the State.
(*See* a.)

3. Archeolodzy nie mogą przechowywać znalezionych przez siebie skarbów w tak skandalicznych warunkach.
– Archaeologists mustn't store their **valuable finds** in such scandalous conditions.
(*See* a.)

4. Zdrowie jest najcenniejszym skarbem człowieka.
– Health is man's most precious **asset**.
(*See* c.)

5. Nasza nowa gosposia jest istnym skarbem.
– Our new maid is a real **treasure**.
(*See* d.)

6. 'Chodź, skarbie', mówił do żony, 'pokaż swoją nową suknię'.
– "Come on, **darling / dear / sweetie**", he said to his wife, "let's see your new dress".
(*See* d.)

7. Chodź do mnie, skarbie, i daj mi buzi.
– Come over here to me, **sweetheart**, and give me a kiss.
(*See d.*)

8. Chłopczyk szybko pobiegł do swego pokoju i przyniósł stamtąd wszystkie swoje skarby – szkiełka, muszelki, kolorowe kamyczki.
– The boy quickly ran to his room and brought out all his **treasures** – bits of glass, seashells, coloured pebbles.
(*See* a.)

Sprawiać, że ...

The Polish phrase 'sprawiać, że' is extremely difficult to translate, mainly, it would seem, because English and Polish have different kinds of syntax.

Here are some sentences containing the Polish phrase 'sprawiać, że ...' and suggested English equivalents.

One can use the English verb **cause** with a direct object, but *not* with the construction **cause that**, e.g.

Wczorajsza ulewa sprawiła, że niektóre ulice tonęły w wodzie.
– Yesterday's torrential rain **caused** serious flooding in some streets.
CORRECT – since the direct object (D.O.) is used
WRONG – One cannot say: ... caused that flooding was serious.

Now we have some correct sentences with no direct equivalent, e.g.

Czysty przypadek sprawił, że dopiero cztery dni później dowiedzieliśmy się o tym wypadku.
– **By sheer chance** we only heard about the accident four days later.

and

Jego poczucie humoru sprawia, że ona jest zawsze w doskonałym nastroju.
– His sense of humour **keeps her** in a constantly good mood.

Other possible ways of translating 'sprawiać, że ...':

lead to sth

Zimowa pogoda sprawiła, że ceny samochodów nieco się obniżyły.
– The winter weather **has led to** a slight fall in car prices.

make

Opady marznącej mżawki sprawiają, że na drogach jest bardzo ślisko.
– Drizzle, freezing as it falls, **is making** the roads very treacherous.

Sztormy na Bałtyku sprawiły, że nasze statki spóźniły się do portu.
– Storms in the Baltic **made** our ships late reaching port.

Taka pogoda sprawia, że ludzie czują się senni.
– This kind of weather **makes** people feel sleepy.

Jego humor, fantazja i zapewne także inne zalety sprawiły, że cieszył się u kobiet zawrotnym powodzeniem.

– His sense of humour, imagination, and no doubt other virtues as well, **made** him a dazzling success with women.

Spraw, aby Tomek sprzątał swój pokój.
– **Make** Tom tidy his room!

owing to

Brak wiadomości sprawia, że nie może on powziąć żadnej decyzji.
– **Owing to** lack of news, he is unable to come to any decision.

Te i inne czynniki sprawiły, że dziś ziemia jest znacznie mniej żyzna.
– **Owing to** these and other factors, the soil is much less fertile today.

put

Ta okropna pogoda sprawia, że jestem w złym humorze.
– This terrible weather **has put me** in a bad mood.

as a result of

Ich skandaliczne zachowanie się sprawiło, że zostali wykluczeni z rozgrywek o Puchar Europy.

– **As a result** of their scandalous behaviour, they were excluded from the European Cup fixtures.

Gwałtowne ulewy sprawiły, że część pól uprawnych została zalana wodą.

– **As a result of** torrential rain, some of the fields were flooded.

Using the present participle:

Wielkie zmęczenie sprawiło, że zasnął natychmiast.

– **Being** very tired, he fell asleep immediately.

Using the past participle:

Odkrycie jej tajemnicy sprawiło, że już nigdy nie mógł czuć się swobodnie w jej towarzystwie.

– **Having discovered** her secret, he was unable ever again to feel at all at ease in her company.

Spuścizna

'Spuścizna' is something a person has left to his heirs after his death. It may be something abstract, or on the other hand something quite tangible, such as a 'spuścizna literacka', or some musical composition, or it might be paintings, or even land or money.

Some examples are given below.

1. Spuścizna tego pisarza jest nam dobrze znana.
– We are all familiar with the work which the writer **left to posterity**.

2. Spuścizna literacka tego pisarza obejmuje kilka powieści historycznych.
– The literary **legacy** left by the writer includes several historical novels.

3. Spuścizna, jaką pozostawił po sobie Mickiewicz, jest przebogata.
– When Mickiewicz died, he left to posterity a magnificent literary **legacy**.

4. Spuścizna literacka tego pisarza obejmuje wiele tomów prozy i poezji.

– The body of literary **work** which this author **left behind** him includes many volumes of prose and poetry.

5. Jan Matejko pozostawił po sobie bogatą spuściznę w postaci obrazów historycznych przedstawiających najważniejsze dzieje Polski.

– Matejko **bequeathed to future generations** a rich collection of his paintings depicting the most important events in Poland's history.

6. Ta jego choroba to spuścizna po beztroskim życiu.

– His illness is / was **the result / legacy** of loose living.

7. Dzisiejsze trudności ekonomiczne są spuścizną polityki rządów poprzednich lat.

– Today's economic difficulties **are the legacy / consequence** of the policies of previous governments.

8. Dzięki spuściźnie po ojcu zbudował sobie piękny dom.

– Thanks to an **inheritance** from his father, he was able to build a fine house.

w Sumie

This phrase may be translated as:

All in all, ...
Altogether, ...
To sum up, ...
Taking everything into consideration, ...

It makes a good beginning to an English sentence.

Sympatyczny

The Polish word 'sympatyczny' and the English word **symphathetic** look very similar to each other, but differ in meaning.

The Polish word 'sympatyczny' means **likeable, amiable, friendly**, while the English word **sympathetic** means **compassionate** – 'współczujący', 'ubolewający', **feeling pity**.

Środki

The most common English equivalent of 'środki' or 'środek' is **means** (i.e. methods, measures, something used to attain something else). Many examples of the word 'środki' occur with an attribute attached, as will be seen below:

środki antykoncepcyjne – **contraceptives**
środki chemiczne – **chemicals**
środki czyszczące – **cleaning materials**
środki doraźne – **emergency measures**
środki lokomocji – **transport, means of transport**
środki masowego przekazu – **the mass media**
środki masowej zagłady – **weapons of mass destruction**
środki nasenne – **sleeping pills**
środki ostrożności – **precautions**
środki przeciwbólowe – **painkillers**
środek przeczyszczający – **purge, laxative**
środek trujący – **poison**
środki upiększające – **beauty aids**

It will be noticed that few of these contain in English the specific word meaning 'środki'.

But in general sentences, the most common equivalents for 'środek, środki' unaccompanied by an attribute are: **means, methods, measures, possibilities, resources**. Here are a few such sentences:

1. Policja zastosuje wszystkie możliwe środki, aby utrzymać porządek publiczny.
– The police will use all **means** in their power to maintain law and order.

2. Mamy zamiar zastosować wszystkie możliwe środki, aby osiągnąć nasz cel.
– We intend to use all possible **means / measures / methods** to attain our aim.

We also find such phrases as:

3. Nie cofać się przed żadnym środkiem działania.
– To stop at nothing.

Cel uświęca środki.
– The end justifies **the means**.

But 'środki' has still other meanings: **money, capital, financial resources, funds**, etc., e.g.

5. Trudno w tych czasach zdobyć środki do życia.
– It is no easy matter these days to make enough **money** to live on.

6. Po wojnie wiele środków przeznaczyliśmy na rozbudowę kluczowych działów przemysłu.
– After the war, we designated large **sums of money** for the expansion of key branches of industry.

7. Nasze środki są tak skromne, że nawet nie możemy marzyć o możliwości wyjazdu na wakacje.
– We're so short of **funds / money** that we can't even think of going away anywhere for a holiday.

Tak więc

The expression 'tak więc' has a number of equivalents in English, although these are very similar to each other in meaning.

Specimen translation:

1. Tak więc razem z ASP miasto posiada osiem wyższych uczelni.
– **Thus** together with the Art College, the city has eight institutions of higher education.

2. Tak więc w najbliższym czasie będzie gościć w naszym kraju gwiazda rocka – Ałła Pugachova.
– **So** before long (in the near future) the rock star Alla Pugachova will visit Poland.

3. Tak więc (w ten sposób) znów wróciliśmy do punktu wyjścia.
– **Thus** we come back to our starting-point.

4. Tak więc po dziesięciu latach daremnych usiłowań, trzeba było zacząć wszystko od początku.
– **So that** after ten years of futile endeavour, we had to start everything from scratch.

5. Tak więc zdecydowałem się pojechać do Paryża.
– **So for these reasons** I decided to go to Paris.

6. Zdajesz się całkowicie nic nie rozumieć, tak więc sądzę, że dalsze prowadzenie naszej rozmowy nie ma sensu.
– You don't seem to understand anything at all, **so** I see no point in continuing our conversation.

7. Tak więc jedynym nasuwającym się wnioskiem jest, że było to morderstwo.
– **Hence** the only reasonable conclusion was that it was murder.

8. Tak więc doszliśmy do końca naszych obrad.
– **That** brings us to the end of our discussion.

9. Tak więc po deszczu poranek był chłodny i wilgotny.
– After the rain, **then**, the morning remained cold and damp.

10. Grzebaliśmy się za długo, tak więc spóźniliśmy się więcej niż godzinę.
– We took too long getting ready and **consegnently / because of that** we were over an hour late.

11. Powiedział 'Żegnaj!' – tak więc zrozumiała, że spotykają się po raz ostatni.
– 'Goodbye', he said, **so** she knew they would never see each other again.

12. Wydaliśmy początkowo za dużo, tak więc wkrótce zabrakło nam pieniędzy.
– At the beginning we spent too much money, **as a result of which** we soon ran short.

Teren

Very often when translating the word 'teren' we can omit its equivalent in English altogether. For example, we can translate:

1. Na terenie Polski
– **In Poland**
Na terenie miasta
– **In the city**

2. Są jeszcze wilki na terenie Bieszczadów.
– There are still wolves **in the Bieszczady**.

3. Na terenie całego kraju zanotowano bardzo wysokie temperatury.
– **In all parts of Poland / All over Poland** temperatures have been very high.

But sometimes 'teren' is translated by words such as **area** or **region** or **premises** or **bounds**.

4. Na naszym terenie ludzie żyją przeważnie z rolnictwa.
– **In our area**, the people mostly make their living from agriculture.

5. Palenie na terenie zakładu wzbronione.
– No smoking **on factory premises**.

6. Dozorca mieszka na terenie fabryki.
– The caretaker lives **on the factory premises**.

7. Wypadek ten nastąpił na terenie szkoły.
– The accident happened **on the school premises**.

8. Nauczyciele są odpowiedzialni za dzieci na terenie szkoły.
– The teachers are responsible for the children **within** school bounds.

9. Na terenie lotniska obowiązuje zakaz palenia.
– Smoking is strictly prohibited **within** airport **limits**.

10. Na terenie lotniska fotografowanie wzbronione!
– No photographs within airport **perimeter**!
– No photographs **beyond this point!**

In the above examples, the word 'teren' is usually followed by a noun in the genetive (possessive) case (dopełniacz), which qualifies the meaning (application) of the word 'teren'.

Sometimes, however, the restriction of 'teren' is indicated by an adjective or adjectival phrase, as may be seen below:

11. Od miesięcy nie było deszczu na terenie nawiedzonym suszą.
– In this **drought-stricken area** there has been no rain for months.

12. Znaleźliśmy się na dzikim, niezbadanym terenie.
– We found ourselves in wild, unexplored **territory**.

In sentences 11 and 12 **area** and **territory** are very vague terms, and could be replaced by **region**, which can often be used as an equivalent, especially in geographical contexts, e.g.

ogromne tereny objęte suszą we wschodniej Afryce
– vast **arid regions** in eastern Africa.

Sometimes the 'teren' referred to belongs to a special kind, e.g.

13. Trzeba mieć przepustkę, aby móc się dostać na teren wojskowy.
– You have to have a pass, before you're allowed into a **military area** (in wartime) / **military** or **restricted area** (in peacetime).

14. Straszne rzeczy działy się na terenach okupowanych przez hitlerowców.
– Terrible things happened in Nazi-occupied **territory**.

15. Nasze tereny myśliwskie leżą ok. 200 km na północ na Warszawy.
– We have **hunting grounds** about 200 km north of Warsaw.

Sometimes 'teren' denotes not an area, but the configuration of the ground, type of land etc.

16. W rajdzie Kair–Kapsztad, na pewno nie wszyscy kierowcy dojadą do mety, bo teren jest wyjątkowo trudny.
– It's unlikely that all the drivers in the Cairo–Capetown Rally will make it to the finish, as the **terrain** is exceptionally difficult.

And finally, there is a very interesting, idiomatic use of the word 'teren'. Let us imagine the following dialogue, taking place in a factory:

Q. Czy Jaś jest? (Czy jest w fabryce?)
– Is Jack in? (Is Jack here?)

A1. Nie, ale jest gdzieś na terenie fabryki.
– No, but he's **somewhere around**. (i.e. in the factory)

A2. Nie. Jest w terenie. Udał się w teren.
– No, he's not here. **He's away**. Meanings: He's not in the factory

at all; neither is he in the vicinity, because he's gone on business either to a different branch of the same factory, or even to another town, possibly for a few days. In all these cases the implication is that, despite being absent, he's doing something in connection with his job.

Notes. Choice of Vocabulary

In sentences with 'teren' it may be useful to note the difference between **area, region, territory, bounds** and **premises**: **area** is a very vague, 'umbrella' term, which therefore is very useful, as it fits many contexts. When it occurs alone (i.e. not followed by a place-name or other noun), we are given no information about its size or shape.

area

Do *not* say **in the area of Poland**, meaning 'na terenie Polski', but simply **in Poland. In the area of ...** often means 'near, in the vicinity of ...' So 'na terenie miasta' should be translated simply as **in the city**. Use the preposition **in**.

region

Region is similar in meaning, but more precise. It is used often in geographical texts. For instance, we can say 'The railways in the **Southern Region** are to be modernised', and 'Greenland is a desolate **region**'. Instead of translating 'na naszym terenie' as **in our region**, it is better to say **in our area**.

premises

Premises can be used when 'teren' means a building and some attached ground, e.g. **school premises, factory premises, hospital premises**. With **premises** we use the preposition **on**, not **in.**

bounds

Bounds really means 'granice', e.g. **within school bounds** means **inside the confines** (granice) of both the school buildings and the ground round them (e.g. the playground). Here we use the preposition **within**.

territory

Territory is a suitable word to use in texts dealing with war and concerning military expansion. A territory is usually a large area, with well-defined boundaries, e.g. 'The German Reich soon extended its **territory** to include Czechoslovakia'.

The word **territory** can also be applied to the life of animals, e.g. 'each animal fiercely defends its own **territory** against all comers'.

Note the following typical errors and their correct version.

WRONG	***RIGHT***
Prepositions:	
on an area –	**in** an area
in the premises –	**on** the premises
north from Warsaw –	north **of** Warsaw
in the area of Poland –	**in** Poland
Vocabulary:	
hunting area –	**hunting ground/s**
smoking is forbidden (too weak) smoking is not allowed (too weak) in the area of the factory –	smoking is **prohibited (on the premises)**
in the area of the city (this may mean: in the vicinity of the city) –	**in the city**
territories under Hitler's occupation –	**Nazi-occupied territory**
a draught-stricken area –	**a drought-stricken area** (spelt with an **o**; draught means 'przeciąg', drought means 'susza')
on the area of the whole country –	**all over Poland / the country, throughout Poland / the country, throughout the whole country, in all parts of the country**

Trzeba, trzeba było

First let us deal with 'trzeba', and then with 'trzeba było'.

The sentences with 'trzeba' are in the present tense, and deal with facts. Unlike some of those with 'trzeba było' they are not conditional.

A. 'Trzeba' (present tense)

1. Trzeba tej Pani powiedzieć, że jej męża zabrano do szpitala.
– She **must** be told that her husband has been taken to hospital. (must – report of factual situation)

2. Trzeba zarabiać więcej, jeżeli się chce podnieść swoją stopę życiową.
– One **must** earn more money if one wants to have a better standard of living.

3. Trzeba zgasić światło, aby dziecko mogło spać.
– Let's put out the light, so the baby can get to sleep. (advice)

4. Trzeba go odwiedzić.
– You **should** go and see him.

5. Trzeba wydawać tylko tyle, ile się ma, aby przetrwać trudny okres.
– One **must** live within one's income, if one wishes to survive hard times.

6. Trzeba uważnie przeanalizować swoje postępowanie, aby móc właścicie je ocenić.
– In order to judge one's actions properly, one **has to** subject them to close scrutiny.

7. Trzeba być bardzo cierpliwym, aby móc uczyć innych.
– You **have to** have a lot of patience, to be able to teach.

8. Pomóc Ci?
– Need any help?
Nie, nie trzeba.
– No, it's all right.
– No, I'm all right. (negative)

With 'trzeba było', a certain amount of doubt and confusion may arise, because the same words may mean different things. For instance, in some cases they tell us something straightforward about facts, whereas in others they may tell us about some conditional situation.

B. *'Trzeba było' (past tense)*

Here are some sentences where the meaning is factual:

1. Trzeba było działać szybko.
– **It was imperative** to act quickly.

2. Trzeba było zapewnić kolonistom dostawy niewolników.
– The colonists **had to** be assured of getting supplies of slaves.

3. Na projekt ten trzeba było poświęcić dużo czasu.
– We **had to** spend a lot of time on that design.

4. Trzeba było przerwać mecz.
– The match **had to** be interrupted.

5. Na wąskiej drodze trzeba było prowadzić samochód bardzo ostrożnie.
– Since we were going along a narrow road, **we had** to drive very carefully.

6. Trzeba było wiele wysiłku, by dobrze go wychować!
– A lot of effort **was needed** to bring him up properly!

7. **Trzeba było** jej powiedzieć, że jej męża zabrano do szpitala.
– She **should have** been told that her husband had been taken to hospital.

8. Trzeba było kupić samochód, aby jeździć nim do pracy.
– We **had to** buy a car, in order to get to work.

9. Ze względu na dużą ilość opadów, trzeba było zrezygnować z dalszych wycieczek w góry.
– In view of the heavy rain, we **had to** give up the idea of further trips into the mountains.

10. Trzeba było szybko wykonać pracę, bo zbliżał się koniec roku.
– We **had to** finish the job quickly, because the end of the year was approaching.

11. Trzeba było wykonać tłumaczenie przed końcem tygodnia.
– We **had to** hand in our translation by the end of the week.

These are straightforward statements of fact, and are translated by means of the simple past tense.

C. 'Trzeba było' (supposition / condition)

Now we come to somewhat more complicated situations, in which we do not have simple fact, but some supposition or condition.

Here are several such sentences:

1. Trzeba było widzieć ten korek uliczny, w którym wczoraj utknąłem.
– You **should have seen** the traffic jam I was stuck in yesterday.
(But you didn't see it.)

This is where the doubts and confusion about meaning arise.

We are sometimes not sure if we are dealing with fact or some condition or supposition, e.g.

2. Trzeba było pić powoli, a nie sparzyłbyś języka.
– You **should have drunk** slowly, and you wouldn't have burnt your tongue. (But you didn't drink slowly.)
(*condition* – **if** you had drunk slowly ...)

3. Trzeba było zakończyć te spory, by wreszcie zapanował u nas spokój.
– We **should have ended** our quarrels, to ensure peace and quiet at last. (But we didn't end them.)
(*advice, condition*)

Note the use of the auxiliary **should**.

Note that some of these sentences are ambiguous. It is not easy to recognise from the outward form whether we are dealing with fact, or with supposition, e.g.

4. Trzeba było zgasić światło, żeby dziecko mogło zasnąć.
Does this mean:
– We **had to** put out the light to let the baby get to sleep,
(*fact*)
or:
– We **should have** put out the light (but we didn't), to let the baby get to sleep.
(*advice*)
or:
– **If we had** put out the light, the baby **would have** got to sleep.
(*condition*)

In these Polish sentences, it is not possible to recognise from the outward form, which is the intended meaning.

5. Trzeba było najpierw pomyśleć, zanim zrobiłeś takie głupstwo!
– You **should have** thought first, before doing such a silly thing!
(*Meaning:* **if you had thought** first, you **would not have done** such a silly thing!)

D. 'Trzeba' (future tense)

1. Podczas pobytu w Paryżu, trzeba będzie koniecznie zwiedzić Luwr.
– When we're in Paris, **we simply must** visit the Louvre.

2. Trzeba, abyś go odwiedził.
– You **should / must** go and see him.

3. Dzieci zostawiły po sobie taki bałagan, iż trzeba będzie sprzątać całe mieszkanie.
– The children have left such a mess, that **we'll have to** clear up the whole flat.

Twórczość (literary)

The following sentence may illustrate how to translate this word:

Książka ta jest bardzo charakterystyczna dla twórczości tego pisarza.
– This book is very characteristic of the author's **work**.

Note the preposition **of**, *not* **for**.

Ubogi; ubodzy

For translating 'ubogi', or its plural 'ubodzy', note the following sentences:

1. Gleba ta jest uboga w minerały.
– The soil there is **poor** in minerals.

Note the preposition **in:** sth is **poor**; be **poor in** sth

2. Pustynia Błędowska jest uboga w szatę roślinną.
– The Błędowo Desert has only **sparse** vegetation.

3. Rejon ten zamieszkuje uboga ludność koczownicza.
– The region is inhabited by a **poor**, nomadic population.

4. Teren ten jest ubogi w wodę.
– This area is **lacking in** water.
– Water is **scarce** in this area.

5. Język tej książki jest ubogi.
– The language of the book **lacks sophistication**.

6. Nowy nauczyciel jest ubogi doświadczeniem.
– The new teacher **lacks** experience / is **lacking** in experience.

7. W tym mieście architektura jest bardzo uboga.
– In this city the architecture is very **plain / primitive / poor / uninteresting**.

8. Chciałby być pisarzem, ale jego język jest ubogi.
– He would like to be a writer, but his language is **not sophisticated enough**.

9. Traktowano ją jak ubogą krewną.
– She was treated like a **poor** relation.

10. Należy pomóc **ubogim**.
– We ought to help the **poor**. (class noun)

Note, for translating 'ubodzy' (plural):

RIGHT – **the poor** (using the adjective alone, as a class noun)
– the **poorer** people
– the **poorer** section of the population
– the **less well-off** section of the population

Note than when 'ubodzy' is translated into English, we often use the comparative form of the adjective (stopień wyższy).

Similarly, when translating 'młode pokolenie' into English, we use the comparative form of the adjective, **the younger generation** (*not* **the young generation**), although when we use the adjective alone, as a class noun, we can say **the young**, e.g.

Wokół nas jest zawsze dużo ubogich.
– The **poor** are always with us.

We also say:

ubodzy duchem
– the **poor** in spirit.

Uczyć się

At first sight the English verb **to learn** would seem to be a satisfactory equivalent for the Polish 'uczyć się'. But if we take a closer look, this conclusion is satisfactory only if we are dealing with an example such as 'uczyć się czegoś' – that is, when 'uczyć się' takes a direct object, as 'uczyć się francuskiego', in other words, when both the Polish verb 'uczyć się' and its proposed English equivalent are in effect transitive verbs.

Nevertheless, in Polish we may encounter 'uczyć się' as an intransitive verb, meaning **to study**, with no direct object, in such phrases as:

Nie mogę iść dziś do kina; muszę zostać w domu i się uczyć.
– I can't go to the cinema today; I have to stay at home and **study**.

But in this sentence the verb **study** is used intransitively, too, which is not quite right. The same situation would have arisen with the verb **learn**, which likewise calls for a direct object. In everyday speech a native speaker would say:

– I have to stay at home and **work**.

Note also:

– I'm working for my exams.

As we have said above, the English **learn** is seldom used as an intransitive verb, although occasionally it does occur, e.g. in such phrases as:

– He did a very foolish thing. He'll never **learn**.

But here it refers to behaviour, not to studying. In such cases, **to learn** means not to acquire some specific **knowledge**, but to modify behaviour through **experience**.

Coming back to 'uczyć się', note the following sentences:

Musiałam całą noc uczyć się do egzaminu. (Note the preposition.)
– I was up all night **studying for** my exam (*not* learning). (Note the preposition.)

Note also:

Tom jest studentem bardzo sumiennym. On dużo się uczy.
– Tom is a very conscientious student. He **works** very hard.

Jeśli będzie uczyć się tak dużo jak obecnie, ma wszelkie szanse zdać egzamin.
– If he carries on **working** as hard as he is now, he will stand a good chance of passing his exam.

Uwarunkowany czymś

Do not translate the above as 'conditioned by sth'. Very occasionally the phrase **conditional on sth else** is encountered, and seems acceptable. Occasionally one can use the phrase **be a condition of sth**.

But by far the best and most reliable translation is: sth **depends on** sth else.

Illustrative sentences

Some illustrative sentences are given below. These are followed by other sentences showing first a wrong translation, and then a good one.

Correct translation

1. Jest to uwarunkowane wieloma czynnikami.
– That **depends on** many factors.

2. Rozwój wymiany Wschód–Zachód uwarunkowany będzie zarówno przesłankami ekonomicznymi, jak i politycznymi.
– Growth of East–West trade will **depend on** both economic and political considerations.

3. Rozwój turystyki uwarunkowany jest istnieniem bazy hotelowej.
– The development of tourism will **depend on** the availability of hotel accommodation.

4. Będzie to uwarunkowane sytuacją.
– That will **depend on** circumstances.

But we can also say:

5. Zawarcie umowy uwarunkowane jest możliwością uzyskania odpowiedniego finansowania.
– The deal **depends on** the availability of finance.

6. Nasz wyjazd jest uwarunkowany możliwościami dewizowymi.
– Whether or not we shall be able to go on our trip abroad will **depend on** whether we have enough foreign currency.

Right and wrong sentences

1. Portugalczycy zdawali sobie sprawę, że powodzenie tej imprezy uwarunkowane będzie przyjazną współpracą z kupcami.
WRONG – The Portuguese realised that the success of this enterprise would be **conditioned by** friendly co-operation with the traders.
RIGHT – The Portuguese realised that the success of this enterprise **depended on / was conditional on** friendly co-operation with the traders.

2. Wiedzieli też, że zakup złota i niewolników uwarunkowany był dostawą na brzegi Afryki wielkich ilości wyrobów żelaznych, mosiężnych i miedzianych.
WRONG – They also knew that the purchase of gold and slaves was **conditioned by** the supply of large quantities of iron, brass, and copper goods to the African coast.
RIGHT – They knew that **in order to be able to** purchase gold and slaves, **they would have to** supply large quantities of iron, brass and copper artefacts to the African coast.

3. Podatki, które płacę, są uwarunkowane moimi dochodami.
WRONG – The taxes I pay are **conditioned by** my income.
RIGHT – The taxes I pay **depend on** the size of my income.

4. Zorganizowanie przyjęcia uwarunkowane było punktualnym przybyciem Pana X do Londynu.

WRONG – Arrangement of the party was **conditioned by** Mr X's arrival in London on time.

RIGHT – Arrangement of the party was **conditional on** Mr X's arrival in London on time.

BETTER – The party was to be held **only if** Mr X arrived in London on time.

BEST – Arrangements for the party **depended on / were subject to** Mr X's arriving in London on time.

5. Wynik tego procesu uwarunkowany będzie wieloma czynnikami.

RIGHT – The outcome of this process **will depend on** many factors.

NEVER translate 'uwarunkowany czymś' as **conditioned by**, but possibly as **conditional on.**

Uzasadniać

Some examples of how to translate this word are given in the following sentences.

1. Jak uzasadniasz swoje prawa do tego domu?

– **On what grounds** do you claim a right to the house?

– **What is the basis of your** claim to the house?

2. W sądzie żona musiała uzasadniać prośbę o rozwód.

– The wife had to **present** to the Court **the grounds** on which she was seeking a divorce.

3. Cel uzasadnia (uświęca) środki.

– The end **justifies** the means.

4. Ta zmiana decyzji uzasadniona była ważnymi względami społecznymi.

– This change of decision was **motivated by** important social considerations.

Uzasadnienie

Now we came to translation of the noun *uzasadnienie*. Here are some specimen sentences.

1. Wkrótce też pojawia się u Europejczyków inne uzasadnienie handlu niewolnikami.
– Shortly afterwards yet another **argument / excuse** for the slave trade was propounded by the Europeans.

2. Moje nadzieje znajdują uzasadnienie w otrzymanych wczoraj wiadomościach.
– My hopes are **based on / founded on** the news we had yesterday.

3. Sądzę, że odmowa Edwarda miała uzasadnienie.
– I imagine **there was good reason for** Edward's refusal.

4. Podejście premiera do problemu ma swoje uzasadnienie.
– The Prime Minister's approach to the problem **is not unwarranted**.

5. Jego złe zachowanie ma uzasadnienie w jego trudnym dzieciństwie.
– The **reasons for** his bad behaviour **can be traced back** to his difficult childhood.
– **The roots of** his bad behaviour can be sought in his difficult childhood.
– His bad behaviour can to some extent be **justified / excused** by his difficult childhood.

6. Nie ma żadnego uzasadnienia twierdzenie, że Kościuszko zostawił zbyt wiele wojska w Warszawie.
– There are no **grounds** for asserting that Kościuszko left too large a proportion of his army in Warsaw.
– There is no **solid evidence** that ...
– We see no **reason** to accept the view that ...

7. Nie wszystkie zjawiska zachodzące w kosmosie znajdują uzasadnienie we współczesnej teorii.
– Not all that has been happening in space can be **explained by** modern theory.

8. (Question on official form asking for visa)

Uzasadnienie prośby o wizę do XYZ:
– What is the **purpose** of your visit to XYZ?

9. Jakie Pan ma uzasadnienie dla swoich poglądów?
– What evidence are your opinions based on?

10. Takie rozumowanie ma swoje uzasadnienie w praktyce.
– Such reasoning **is borne out by** practice.

11. Uzasadnienie do ustawy.
– **Preamble** to a statute.

Warunki

In Polish, 'warunki' implies a variety of meanings. When it occurs alone, or in the phrase 'w tych warunkach', we may find its English equivalent among the following: **conditions, circumstances, terms, environment, physique** (body build). Some sample sentences are given below.

I. One meaning which seems strange to English ears is: **physique, type of body, physical build**, etc., e.g.

1. Szewińska miała wspaniałe warunki do biegania,

meaning that she had long legs, the kind of body that enabled her to run well, and win many races:

– Szewińska had an ideal **build / type of body / physique** for running.

2. Aktor ten ma wspaniałe warunki do uprawiania swego zawodu.
– The actor is lucky in having such good **looks**.

In the above sentences, 'warunki' applies to a person. But more commonly, 'warunki' refers to external, often physical conditions, e.g.

3. Ich warunki mieszkaniowe są okropne.
– Their living **conditions** are dreadful.

4. Tu jest zbyt wielki hałas. Nie mogę pracować w tych warunkach.
– It's too noisy here. I can't work in such **conditions**.

Sometimes such a sentence can be translated less literally, and possibly more colloquially:

Ale hałas! W tych warunkach nie mogę pracować!
– What a din! **With such a row going on**, how can anyone be expected to get any work done!

When 'warunki' are even more physical, we could translate this word as **environment**, e.g.

5. W szklarni było dość wilgotno, bardzo ciepło, było dużo światła. W tych warunkach wegetacja roślin postępowała bardzo szybko.
– It was very warm, humid, and very light in the glasshouse, so in **such an environment** plant growth was very rapid.

When the 'warunki' are not so purely physical, but include, say, psychological elements, **circumstances** is a very appropriate word, e.g.

6. W tych warunkach (e.g. śmierć matki, brak pieniędzy, choroba, etc.), nie mógł koncentrować się na studiach.
– **In these circumstances** (his mother's death, lack of money, illness, etc.), he couldn't concentrate on his work.

Sometimes we can omit the explicit word for **conditions** or **circumstances**, e.g.

7. Nie mieliśmy benzyny. Poza tym, było szalenie zimno. W tych warunkach musieliśmy więc zrezygnować z dalszego udziału w rajdzie.
– We had run out of petrol and apart from that it was freezing cold. **Consequently** we had no alternative but to withdraw from the rally.

Other phrases, too, can be used to express 'w tych warunkach', e.g.

Therefore / In view of the circumstances / As things are / If that is so / Such the case being / Since that is the position, nothing more can be done.

II. But 'warunki' can have an abstract meaning, too. It may mean **terms**, i.e. conditions that must be met before something else can happen. Here are some examples:

8. Zanim podpiszemy umowę, musimy zapoznać się z jej warunkami.
– Before we sign the contract, we must study its **terms**. (conditions)

9. Na pewno warunki będą łagodne.
– The **terms** will certainly be acceptable.

10. Wczoraj ustaliliśmy już warunki sprzedaży.
– Yesterday we agreed the **conditions** of sale. ('conditions of sale', is a term)

III. Lastly, we have 'warunki atmosferyczne', meaning **weather**:

11. Sądzimy, z wysokim stopniem prawdopodobieństwa, że ostatnia groźna katastrofa lotnicza w dużej mierze spowodowana była wyjątkowo złymi warunkami atmosferycznymi.
– We are quite convinced that the recent terrible air disaster was largely due to the **exceptionally bad weather**.
Note: we can also say: 'due to the **exceptionally bad weather conditions**, but in English the addition of the word **conditions** is superfluous.

Wiadomo, że ...

The following, largely synonymous phrases are useful when translating 'wiadomo, że ...'. They generally come at the beginning of a sentence. They comprise: **Of course, Obviously, It's clear that..., It's obvious that..., We all know that..., It's common knowledge that..., Everybody / Everyone knows that..., It's a well-known fact that...**

Some sentences illustrating usage of these phrases are given below:

1. Wiadomo, że dziś jest za późno, aby robić zakupy, bo sklepy zamykają o 5.
– **Of course / Obviously** it's too late to do the shopping today, because the shops close at 5.

2. Wiadomo, że Andrzej powinien rzucić palenie.
– **It's clear / It's obvious** that Andrew should give up smoking.

3. Wiadomo, że nigdy dotąd przywódcy tych krajów nie doszli do porozumienia.
– **It's common knowledge that** the leaders of these countries have never yet managed to reach agreement.
– The leaders of these countries, **as we know**, have never yet managed to reach agreement.

4. Wiadomo, że Filip bardzo przeżył śmierć swojej matki.
– **Everyone knows that** Philip felt his mother's death very keenly.

5. Powszechnie wiadomo, że aby znać jakiś język, trzeba się uczyć systematycznie.
– **It's a well-known fact that / Everybody knows that** if you want to speak a language well, you have to learn it systematically.

Negative: 'nie wiadomo', 'nie wiadomo jeszcze':

6. Nie wiadomo jeszcze, ile to ma kosztować.
– **We don't know yet** how much it will cost.

7. Nie wiadomo jeszcze, kto będzie premierem.
– **No-one knows yet** who will be Prime Minister.

8. Nie wiadomo jeszcze, jakie są wyniki wyborów.
– The election results **are not known yet**.

9. W dalszym ciągu nie wiadomo, jakie są wyniki wyborów.
– We're still **in the dark** as to the election results.

10. Nie wiadomo jeszcze, kto będzie kapitanem drużyny.
– **It's not yet known** who is to be captain of the team.
– **We don't yet know...**

jak Wiadomo

The only differences between the sentences given here, and the previous group, is the presence of 'jak' (**as**), which nevertheless may alter the sentence construction. When translating sentences containing the phrase 'jak wiadomo', this may be rendered as **as we all know, as is common knowledge, as everyone knows**, etc., e.g.

1. Jak wszystkim wiadomo, druga wojna światowa wybuchła w 1939 r.
– World War II, **as we all know,** broke out in 1939.
as is common knowledge...
as everyone knows...

Note that although these English phrases beginning with **as** can be placed (as in Polish) at the beginning of the sentence, it is generally more elegant to put them in second place – that is, after the subject of the sentence. Such a phrase then appears in parenthesis, and must be flanked by commas, as in sentence 1 above, or as in sentence 2 below:

2. Pierwsza próba, jak wiadomo, nie powiodła się.
– The first attempt, **as everyone knows**, was a failure.

Here are a few examples of right and wrong usage:

WRONG – One must never say: As it is well known, ... or: As it is common knowledge, ... One must omit either **as**, or **it**.

RIGHT – **It is well known that ...**, or: **It is common knowledge that ...** (no comma before **that**), or, also correct: **As is well known, ...** or: **As is commonly known, ...** (both phrases followed by a comma, and not followed by the word **that**).

Here are some Polish sentences beginning with 'jak wiadomo'. In the English translation, the sequence of the elements of the sentence varies. (Note the position of the English translation of 'jak wiadomo'.)

1. Jak każdemu wiadomo, Kolumb odkrył Amerykę w 1492 r.
– **As everybody knows,** Columbus discovered America in 1492, or:
– Columbus, **as everybody knows**, discovered America in 1492.

2. Jak wiadomo, palenie papierosów może spowodować raka.
– **It is a well-known fact** that cigarette-smoking may lead to cancer, or:
– Smoking, **as we all know**, may lead to cancer.

3. Jak wiadomo, nie ma innego wyboru, i musimy się na to zgodzić.
– **Clearly** we have no other choice, so we must accept it, or:
– **As we all know**, there is no other choice, so we must accept it.

4. Jak wiadomo, nie uda się zakończyć budowy metra ani w tym roku, ani w następnym.
– **As is now generally known**, the construction of the underground won't be completed either this year or next.

Właśnie

'Właśnie' does not constitute a basic element of any sentence in which it occurs. But it is a very handy instrument adding to and clarifying the meaning of the sentence. Thus 'właśnie' has several possible functions – such as identifying, pinpointing, affirming, clarifying and emphasizing – by means of which the meaning of the sentence is enriched.

English words associated with the meaning of 'właśnie' are: **just** (time, e.g. 'właśnie miałem wyjść' – 'I was **just about** to go out'); **just** (pinpointing, identifying, e.g. 'właśnie osoba, którą chciałem spotkać' – '**just** the person I wanted to see' or 'właśnie takiego szukałem' – 'the **very** thing', 'this is the **very thing I was looking for**', '**it was just the** kind I wanted'); **exactly** how, **exactly** who, **exactly** what; **precise, precisely**: that was **precisely** my intention'; 'the librarian found **precisely** the quotation I needed'; **particular**: 'właśnie w tym momencie' – 'at that **particular** moment my attention was distracted'.

'Właśnie' is also sometimes used in isolation, as a single-word response confirming a remark made by some other person, e.g.

Strasznie zimno dzisiaj, prawda?
– Terribly cold today, istn't it?
Właśnie!
In English this reponse would be:
– **Yes, it is**, or:
– **Yes, isn't it?**

Let us now look at some sentences illustrating these points.

Pinpointing time:

Gdzie są nasi znajomi?
Tu są! Właśnie przyszli!
– Where are our friends?
– Here they are! They've **just** come!

Czy skończyłeś już czytać książkę, którą ci pożyczyłem?
Tak, właśnie wczoraj ją skończyłem i chciałem ci ją oddać.
– Have you finished the book I lent you?
– Yes, **in fact**. I **just** finished it yesterday, and was going to give it back to you.

Właśnie miałem zadzwonić do twego ojca, kiedy on zadzwonił do mnie.
– I was **just about to** phone your father, when he phoned me.

Here **just** means **at the very moment** when...

Now we have **just** meaning **manner, exactly, precisely**:

Tak właśnie myślałem.
– **Just** as I thought!

Pinpointing:

Właśnie pana chciałem zobaczyć!
– You're **just** the person I wanted to see!
– You're the **very** person I wanted to see!
– You're **precisely** the person I wanted to see!

As well as 'This is **just** the kind of coat I've been looking for', one can also say:

– This is **exactly** the kind of coat I've been looking for!
– This is the **very kind** of coat I've been looking for!

In an identity parade we may hear: 'właśnie on', meaning:

– The man at the end of the line' is the **very one** I saw yesterday at the scene of the burglary.

In a discussion about books, one person says:

You've read a lot of Evelyn Waugh's books. Do you know 'Brideshead Revisited'?
And his friend says:
– No, I haven't read that **particular** one., i.e.
'Nie, właśnie tej książki nie czytałem.'

Lastly, an instance of *emphasis*:

– The Sunday Times lost its case because the Law Lords applied the pre-judgment test, and it was **that** which was the issue at Strasbourg, and it was **that** which was condemned by the Strasbourg Court ...

In Polish, this would be 'właśnie to ...'

Włącznie

I. *Time*

In translating 'włącznie', when specific dates (days or months) are mentioned, we can use the word **including** or **inclusive**, e.g.

1. Urząd Pocztowy będzie nieczynny do 21 stycznia włącznie.
– The Post Office will be closed up to and including January 21st.

2. Ferie świąteczne ustalono na okres od 20 grudnia do 6 stycznia włącznie.
– The Christmas holidays are from Dec 20th to Jan 6th **inclusive**.

When no actual dates of days or months are mentioned, but only periods, centuries, etc., use the phrase:

– from the beginning of ... up to the end of ... or:
– from the beginning to the end of the ... century

3. Okres powodzenia gospodarczego trwał w tym kraju do ostatniego roku stulecia włącznie.
– Economic prosperity in the country lasted right up until the end of the century.

4. od XV do XVII wieku włącznie
– from the fifteenth **right through to** the end of the seventeenth century

5. To spowoduje zmiany w programach naszych audycji radiowych do świąt Bożego Narodzenia włącznie.
– This will cause disruptions in our radio programmes till **after Christmas**.

6. Proszę oddać prace pisemne do przyszłego czwartku włącznie.
– Please hand in your homework **by** next Thursday / or: **not later than** next Thursday / or: by Thursday **at the latest.**

II. *Not time*

1. Włącznie z ASP, Warszawa posiada osiem wyższych uczelni.
– **Counting** the Academy of Fine Art, Warsaw has eight centres of higher education.

2. W czasie panującego głodu, wielbłąd gotów jest jeść wszystko, włącznie z mięsem i rybami.
– In time of famine, the camel is prepared to eat absolutely anything, **including** meat and fish.

3. Komorne wynosi 700 złotych miesięcznie, łącznie z opłatą za gaz i światło.
– **Altogether** the rent is 700 zlotys per month **including** gas and electricity.

4. Dzienny koszt hotelu za jedną osobę wynosi £ 40, łącznie z wyżywieniem.
– The **all-in / all-inclusive rate** for the hotel is £ 40 per person per day.

Wobec takiego stanu rzeczy

When translating this phrase, one has quite a large number of equivalents to choose from. The best translation is: '**in** these / those circumstances' (N.B. **under** these circumstances is ***WRONG***). But we also have: 'if that is the situation' or: 'in this / that situation', 'since this is the position', 'as things now stand', things being as they are', 'in the present state of affairs', 'if that is the case', 'in that case', 'therefore', 'thus', 'hence', 'consequently', 'in view of the way things have turned out', 'in view of the facts', 'in view of circumstances', 'with these facts in mind'.

Here are some specimen sentences:

1. Wobec takiego stanu rzeczy postanowiliśmy zwrócić się o pomoc do naszego konsulatu.
– **In this situation** we decided to apply to the Consulate for help.

2. Wobec takiego stanu rzeczy radziłbym wycofać się z tego przedsięwzięcia.
– **In these circumstances** I would advise you to withdraw from the scheme.

Note ***WRONG:*** **Under** these circumstances...

3. Wobec takiego stanu rzeczy nie pozostaje nic innego, tylko wyjechać.
– **Things being as they are**, only one course of action remains open to us – to leave immediately.

4. Wobec takiego stanu rzeczy muszę niestety zerwać naszą umowę.
– **In the present circumstances**, I am unfortunately compelled to break off our agreement.

5. Wobec takiego stanu rzeczy nie możemy sobie pozwolić na kupno nowego samochodu.
– **In the present state of affairs**, we cannot afford to buy a new car.

6. Wobec takiego stanu rzeczy musieli sprzedać dom.
– **In view of the situation**, they had to sell their house.

7. Wobec takiego stanu rzeczy pozostało mi tylko podać się do dymisji.
– **At this juncture**, I had no choice but to resign.

8. Jasne było, że rokowania się załamały. Wobec takiego stanu rzeczy ONZ podjęła próby mediacyjne.
– It was clear that negotiations had broken down. **Therefore** the United Nations began attempts at mediation.

9. Wobec takiego stanu rzeczy przewodniczący złożył rezygnację.
– **In view of the circumstances**, the chairman tendered his resignation.

10. Wobec takiego stanu rzeczy trzeba jak najwcześniej podjąć jakąś decyzję.
– **Things have come to such a pass**, that a decision needs to be taken as quickly as possible.

11. Wobec takiego stanu rzeczy musieliśmy zrezygnować z naszych planów.
– **In view of the way things turned out**, we had to give up our plans.

12. Działaliście bez porozumienia ze mną. Wobec takiego stanu rzeczy nie biorę odpowiedzialności za to, co się stanie.
– You acted without consulting me at all. **Consequently**, I can take no responsibility for anything that may happen.

13. Wobec takiego stanu rzeczy nie będę ukrywał, że warunki pracy w Pańskiej firmie mi nie odpowiadają.
– **In view of the facts**, I must confess that I am not impressed with the atmosphere in your factory.

Wskazać, wskazywać

Note the following examples:

I. *Physical*

1. Igła kompasu zawsze wskazuje północ.
– The needle of the compass always **points north**.

2. Strzałka wskazująca w górę prowadzi do poczekalni.
– The arrow **pointing upwards** leads to the waiting-room.

Point to

3. Kobieta wskazywała palcem mężczyznę, który według niej ukradł jej torebkę.
– The woman **pointed to** (v.prep.) the man who, according to her, had stolen her handbag.

Point out

4. Kobieta wskazywała mężczyznę, który według niej ukradł jej torebkę.
– The woman **pointed out** (v.adv.) the man who, according to her, had stolen her handbag.

Point at

5. Mama wskazała na zegar i przypomniała dzieciom, że już czas spać.
– Mummy **pointed at** (v.prep.) the clock, and reminded the children that it was time to go to bed.

II. *Figurative*

When the meaning is figurative, and when the subject is a person, translate 'wskazywać na coś' as: a) **point out**, or b) **draw attention to sth**, e.g.

6. Premier wskazał na korzyści płynące z przedstawionego planu.
– The Prime Minister **pointed out** (v.adv.) / **drew attention to** the advantages of the plan.

7. Lekarz wskazywał na znaczenie właściwego odżywiania.
– The doctor **pointed out** (v.adv.) / **drew attention to** the importance of a proper diet.

Note the pattern:

Person: **point out / draw attention to** – the advantages of sth / the importance of sth / the dangers of sth / the necessity for sth / the need for sth.

But if the subject of 'wskazywać' is not a person but a thing, translate 'wskazywać' as **point to** or **indicate**, e.g.

8. Poziom czerwonych ciałek wskazywał na anemię.
– The level of red blood corpuscles **pointed to / indicated** anaemia.

Note the collocations:

point to / indicate – a disease

9. Zachowanie jego wskazuje na to, że jest naiwny.
– His behaviour **indicates** that he is naive.

10. Drogowskazy wskazywały na to, że mamy skręcić w prawo.
– The signposts **said** we should turn right.

11. Wzrost i waga dziecka wskazywały na niedorozwój fizyczny.
– The child's height and weight **showed / indicated that** he was physically underdeveloped.

Negative indications ('nie wskazywać na coś')

12. Nic nie wskazywało na to, że przyjdzie.
– There was nothing to **suggest** that he would come.

13. Nic nie wskazywało na to, że on jest chory.
– There were **no signs** of illness at all.
– There was nothing at all to **suggest / indicate** that he was ill.

14. Nic nie wskazywało na to, że jest coś nie w porządku.
– There was **not the slightest hint** that there was anything wrong.

III. *Idiomatic*

15. Termometr wskazuje –10°C.
– The thermometer **is at** –10°C.

IV. *Information*

16. Czy Pan byłby tak uprzejmy wskazać mi drogę?
– Could you **tell me / show me** the way?

17. Czy Pan może mi wskazać najlepszą metodę?
– Can you **tell me / show me** the best method?

18. Wskazał najlepszą metodę na to.
– He **indicated / demonstrated** the best way to do it.

Note the collocations:
show sb – the way (droga)
tell sb – the method
indicate – the way to do sth (sposób).

V. *Terms (Warunki, wymagania)*

19. Wyrażamy nadzieję, że Panowie zaakceptują warunki przedstawione w naszej ofercie.
– We hope you will accept the terms **set out / given / indicated / specified** in our offer.

Note the collocations:
set out / indicate / give (mention) / **specify** – the terms

Wspomnieć (należy wspomnieć)

Some of the English words and phrases given below may be found useful in translating the Polish phrase 'należy wspomnieć'.

They include:

1. **remember, recall, recollect, call to mind,**
2. **mention, record sth,**
3. **We must not forget..., One must bear in mind / keep in mind / keep in view,**
4. **One cannot pass over in silence...**

Here are some sentences:

1. Należy wspomnieć, że podpisanie tego układu ma duże znaczenie.
– **It should be mentioned / It should be pointed out / It should be borne in mind / It should be remembered** that the signing of this pact is of great significance.

2. Powiedziałem już chyba wszystko. Można jednak wspomnieć, że są niezłe szanse na to, iż obecna sytuacja da się zmienić.
– I think I have said all there is to say. But perhaps **one could add** that there is a fairly good chance that the present situation can be changed.

3. Należy również wspomnieć, że dom ten był przez pewien czas własnością rodziny Potockich.
– **Another fact worth recalling** is that for a time the house belonged to the Potocki family.

4. Należy tu wspomnieć o osiągnięciach naszego profesora.
– **A word should be said here** about our professor's achievements.
– **It may be apt here** to say something about the professor's achievements.
– This is **an apt moment to say something about** the professor's achievements.

5. Mówiąc o historii lingwistyki, nie sposób nie wspomnieć o Profesorze AB.
– **One cannot talk of** the history of linguistics **without saying something about** Professor AB.
– In speaking of the history of linguistics, **one cannot pass over the name of** Professor AB.

6. Mówiąc o Powstaniu Warszawskim, należy wspomnieć o bohaterskiej pomocy mieszkańców miasta w walce z okupantem.
– When speaking about the Warsaw Rising, it is **only fitting to call to mind** the heroic support given by the townspeople in fighting the Germans.
– In speaking about the Warsaw Rising, **one must not forget ...**

7. Należy również wspomnieć, że praca jej wykonana została samodzielnie.
– **Another fact worth remembering** is that the work was all done by herself.
– **It must also be borne in mind** that ...
– **We must not forget to mention too, the fact** that ...

Wykluczone, Nie jest wykluczone, że ...

Note the following sentences:

1. W naszym zawodzie pomyłka jest wykluczona.
– In our profession, error is **out of the question**.
2. Udział cudzoziemców w tym spotkaniu jest wykluczony.
– Foreigners are **not allowed** to attend the meeting.
3. Zawsze był wykluczony z naszego towarzystwa.
– He was always **excluded** from our company.
4. Był wykluczony z naszego klubu.
– He was **blackballed** from membership of our club.
5. Wykluczone wszelkie ryzyko.
– All risk has been **eliminated**.

Nie jest wykluczone, że ...

1. Nie jest wykluczone, że nastąpi nawrót choroby.
– We cannot **rule out** the possibility of a relaps.
– It is **quite possible** that the illness will recur.

2. Nie jest jednak wykluczone, że zebranie odbędzie się w późniejszym terminie.
– Nevertheless it is **quite possible** that the meeting will be held at a later date.
– Nevertheless the meeting **may possibly be held** at a later date.
– It **can't be said for certain**, however, that the meeting will not be held later.

3. Nie jest wykluczone, że operacja zostanie powtórzona.
– The patient **may have to** undergo a second operation.
– The **possibility** of a second operation **cannot be ruled out**.
– The **necessity** for a second operation **cannot be ruled out**.

4. Nie jest wykluczone, że śmierć spowodowana była nadużyciem środków nasennych.
– **One cannot exclude the possibility that** death was caused by an overdose of sleeping pills.
– **It may well be the case that** death was caused by an overdose of sleeping pills.

5. Nie jest wykluczone, że powodem tej choroby była brudna woda.
– **It may well be that** contaminated water was the cause of the illness.
– **It is quite possible that ...**
– **It is not out of the question** that ...
– **It is not beyond the bounds of possibility that ...**
– **We cannot rule out** the possibility of contaminated water having been the cause of the illness.

6. Nawet nie jest wykluczone, że zaszła pomyłka.
– **There may even have been** an error.

7. Nie jest wykluczone, że w każdym innym przypadku pokusiłbym się o inne określenie.
– **Quite possibly** in every other case I should be tempted to call it something different.

Wymowny

Here is a mini-glossary to help with the translation of 'wymowny'.

'Wymowny', when used in connection with the following words, may be translated as follows:

Evidence (situation) – Adj. **clear, plain**

Expression / eyes – Phrases: **Her expression / eyes** spoke volumes.

Facts – Adj. **clear, clear-cut, convincing, evident, manifest, palpable, plain, significant, transparent, unambiguous**. Suitable phrase: **The facts speak for themselves. / The facts say a lot**.

Gesture – Adj. **expressive, graphic, significant**

Look (n.) (give sb ~ look) – **eloquent, expressive, meaning, meaningful, plain, significant, unmistakable**

Look at sb. (v.) – **meaningfully**

Situation – (v.) **be clear, be plain**.

Here are some sentences:

1. Fakty były wymowne.
– The facts **spoke for themselves**.

2. Fakty były na tyle wymowne, że nie pozostało nam nic innego jak wyjechać z miasta.
– The evidence was so **plain** that we had no recourse but to leave town.

3. Nie rozumieliśmy słów przybyszy, jednak ich gesty były tak wymowne, że doskonale określały sytuację.
– We did not understand the newcomers' words, but their gestures were so **expressive** that they explained the situation perfectly.

4. Kobieta spojrzała na męża wymownie.
– The woman **gave** her husband a **meaning look**.

5. Wyraz jej oczu był wymowny.
– Her eyes **spoke volumes**.

6. Fakt, że został on jednomyślnie mianowany na to stanowisko, jest wielce wymowny.
– The fact that he was unanimously appointed to the job **says a lot**.

7. W odpowiedzi na to pytanie uczynił tylko wymowny gest.
– His only answer to that question was **a shrug of the shoulders / a significant gesture**.

8. Fakt ten jest bardzo wymowny.
– That fact is a very **significant** one.

9. Wymowny gest naszego gospodarza dał nam do zrozumienia, że już czas wyjść.
– Our host's **gesture** indicated to us in no uncertain terms that it was high time for us to leave.

Wynająć

The main two English words corresponding to 'wynająć' are: **to rent** and **to hire**.

The first problem with the Polish word is that it can mean either **rent something to** use oneself, or **rent something for** someone else to use. One must simply guess from the context, e.g.

Mamy zamiar wynająć dla siebie mały domek nad morzem na dwa miesiące.
– We want to **rent** a small house (for our own use) for a couple of months in the summer.

Mamy zamiar wynająć komuś nasz mały domek nad morzem w lecie.
– We intend to **let** it (to someone else).

In the first case, we would say:

We want to **rent** it (i.e. **from** somebody else).

We could say, informally:

We would like to **take** a small house for a month or so.

Rent is a word we can use in both directions, e.g. to rent a house **from** somebody, or rent **to** sb., e.g.: 'Since we were to be away, and didn't want the house to be empty, we've rented it **to** a nice couple for six weeks.' But in the sense of making it available to somebody temporarily, it is more usual to use the word **let** rather than **rent**. We are talking here about the verb **to let**. But **let** can also be a noun, e.g.

Do you want a long **let** or a short **let**?

The next question is whether to use **rent** or **hire**. The choice will depend on the collocating noun. We use **rent** with some nouns and **hire** with others.

We tend to **rent** immovables, such as a house, a hall, a cottage, but also appliances such as a fridge, a TV-set. We can even **rent a car**, as the advertisements say, but it is more usual to **hire** a car.

We can also **hire** something to wear, such as: a wedding dress, a theatrical costume, a dinner jacket, ski equipment, a graduation gown.

We can **rent** a canoe, a house-boat, a yacht.

One can also **hire** certain people, e.g.

some labourers to sink a well,
a gardener to do the garden, a bodyguard to protect us,
a lawyer to advise us,
a detective to investigate sth,
but not a doctor (we consult a doctor).

Wynika, że ...

Look at the following sentences:

1. W tej teorii jedno wynika logicznie z drugiego.
– In this theory one thing **follows** logically from another.

2. Wszystko wiąże się ze sobą, a jedno wynika z drugiego.
– Everything is connected, and one thing **follows** logically from another.

3. Ostatni pożar w tamtej fabryce chemicznej wynikł z nieostrożności personelu.
– The recent fire in the chemical works **was caused by / was due to** negligence on the part of the employees.
– The recent fire in the chemical works **resulted from** negligence on the part of the employees.

4. Wynika z tego jeden logiczny wniosek.
– **From that**, there is only one logical **conclusion to be drawn**.

5. (*Negative:*) Z jego słów nic nie wynika.
– Nothing clear **emerges from what he said**.

6. Zobaczymy później, co z tego wyniknie.
– We'll see later what **will come of it**.

7. Polityka monopolizowania handlu z Afryką czy z Indiami wynikała zresztą z zupełnie słusznych przesłanek gospodarczych.
– But in point of fact, this policy of trying to gain a monopoly of trade with Africa or India **was based on** perfectly sound economic premisses / **stemmed from** perfectly sound economic premisses.

8. (*Negative:*) Z tego, co powiedziałeś, niekoniecznie wynika, że twój przyjaciel źle zrobił.
– From what you have said, **it does not necessarily follow** that your friend did the wrong thing.

9. Z ostatnich doniesień z Bliskiego Wschodu wynika, że napięcie utrzymuje się nadal.
– **According to** the latest reports from the Middle East, tension is still high.

10. Z twych słów wynika, że nie jesteś zadowolony, iż wtrącam się w twoje sprawy.
– From your remarks **it is obvious / clear that** you resent my interfering in your affairs.

11. Wynika z tego, że w każdej chwili możemy liczyć się z eksmisją z tego mieszkania.
– So **it looks as if** we might at any moment be evicted from our flat.

12. Wynika z tego, że było to tylko nieporozumienie.
RIGHT – It **turns out** that it was just a misunderstanding.
WRONG – It **ensues** that it was just a misunderstanding.

13. Z jego wypowiedzi wynika, że nie mieliście racji.
– From what he says, **it is evident** that you were wrong.
– From what he said, **it seems that** ...

14. Z tego wynika, że nie można zwiedzać Muzeum Narodowego w poniedziałki.
RIGHT – **That means that** the National Museum is not open on Mondays.
WRONG – **It results that** the National Museum is not open on Mondays.

15. Z różnych wzmianek w gazetach wynika niezbicie, że ...
– **From** various references in the newspapers, **it is absolutely clear that ...**

16. Ze statystyk włoskich urzędów celnych wynika, że ...
– Italian customs statistics **show that ...**

17. Z tego wynika, że miał on rację.
– **That shows that ... / It only goes to show that ... / So it turns out that** ... / **That means** he was right.

18. Z tych faktów wynika, że ...
– From these facts **it may be concluded** that ...
– These facts **demonstrate** that ...

19. (*Negative:*) Z tego, co powiedziałeś, nie wynika, że twój przyjaciel jest chory.
– From what you said, **it does not follow** that your friend is ill.
– What you said **does not necessarily mean** that your friend is ill.

20. Z moich doświadczeń wynika, że czasami takie rzeczy się zdarzają.
– **It is my experience that** sometimes such things do happen.

21. Z kroniki anglosaskiej wynika, że już w 418 r. Rzymianie ukryli w ziemi większość skarbów znajdujących się w Brytanii.
– The Anglo-Saxon chronicle **tells us** that as early as 418 A.D. the Romans had already buried most of the treasures then existing in Britain.

jak z tego Wynika

Note the following sentences, especially the deliberately wrong translations, so that such mistakes can be avoided.

1. Jak z tego wynika, musimy sami to zrobić.
– **That means** we'll have to do it ourselves.

2. Jak z tych rachunków wynika, wina nie leży po naszej stronie.
RIGHT – **As one can see** from the accounts, the fault does not lie with us.
RIGHT – **According to** the accounts ...
WRONG – As it appears from the accounts, ...

3. Jak z tego wynika, on musiał kłamać.
RIGHT – **So** he must have lied.
RIGHT – **So the conclusion is that** ...
WRONG – As it appears from it ...

4. Jak z tego wynika, on miał rację.
RIGHT – **From what we know now, it appears** he was right.
WRONG – It comes out that he was right.

5. Jak z tego wynika, trzeba będzie jeszcze trochę poczekać.
RIGHT – **If that is the case**, we'll have to wait a little longer.
WRONG – It results from it, that we'll have to wait a little longer.

6. Jak z tego wynika, należy zmienić nasze plany.
RIGHT – **That means** we'll have to change / amend our plans.

7. Jak z tego wynika, nie masz szans zdać pomyślnie tych egzaminów.
RIGHT – **If that is the case**, then you really have no hope of passing the exams.
WRONG – As results from that ...

8. Jak z tego wynika, nasze bilety uprawniają nas do zwiedzania w tym samym dniu kilku oddziałów Muzeum Narodowego.
RIGHT – **That means that** our tickets entitle us to visit several parts of the National Museum on the same day.
WRONG – As it results, our tickets entitle us to visit several parts of the National Museum on the same day.

9. Jak z tego wynika, nie można liczyć na poprawę.
RIGHT – **So** we can't count on any improvement.

10. Jak wynika z zachodnich źródeł, Anglia wyraziła zgodę na przystąpienie do europejskiego konsorcjum produkującego airbusy z Francją i Niemcami.
RIGHT – **According to** Western sources, Britain has agreed to join the European Airbus Consortium along with France and Germany.
WRONG – As proceeds from Western sources, Britain has agreed ...

Wyższe uczelnie

The Polish term 'wyższe uczelnie' is wider than any single one of the English words such as **university, college, institutions of further education, institutions of higher education, academic institutions**. Generally speaking, the word 'wyższa uczelnia' in Polish could be applied to any educational establishment teaching students above the High School level. English has no such *basket* term. And there is immense differentiation among the separate teaching institutions that make up the items in the basket – such as an Oxford or Cambridge college, or a teacher's training college, or an art college, or college of domestic science, etc., in which students end up with a degree or diploma. So it is not easy to find a collective term. Here are some sentences:

1. Miasto posiada osiem wyższych uczelni.
– The city has eight **institutions of higher education**.

2. Liczba wyższych uczelni w naszym kraju nadal wzrasta.
– In Poland the number of **institutions of further and higher education** is still increasing.

3. Dokument ten uprawnia do starania się o przyjęcie na każdą wyższą uczelnię.
– This document entitles one to apply for admission to any **university or college**.

4. Tylko ci, którzy zdali egzamin, zostaną studentami wyższej uczelni.
– Only those who pass the exam will get into **university**.

5. Wyższe uczelnie opuszczają tysiące wykształconych młodych ludzi.
– **The universities** turn out thousands of educated young poeple.

6. Każda wyższa uczelnia powinna wydawać czasopismo zajmujące się jej problemami.
– Every **university or college** should publish a magazine dealing with its own problems and interests.

7. Ponieważ Marek był wszechstronnie uzdolniony, zastanawiał się, na której z wyższych uczelni podjąć studia.
– Since Mark was good at everything, he wondered which **university** he should apply to.

Zabytek / Zabytki

The available monolingual and bilingual dictionaries are of only limited help when it comes to translating 'zabytek / zabytki' into English.

One problem is that there would appear to be more English equivalents than are given in the existing bilingual dictionaries. Some suggestions as to these are given below.

Another problem that arises with the translation of this word is that it means diverse things in Polish: buildings, perhaps also statues and monuments (immovables); works of art such as paintings, smaller sculptures, religious paraphernalia, etc. (movables); or the whole body of treasures of all kinds that come down to a nation from the past; or simply something valuable that has survived from the past. Thus our first task as translators is to decide just exactly what is meant by 'zabytek / zabytki' in the given Polish text, for this will determine our choice of the English equivalent.

As has been said already, our next step should be to try to visualise what is meant by the Polish text, and to convey in English the picture in our mind's eye. This is better than mechanically translating the Polish word into some English equivalent. The use of English texts as patterns is greatly recommended. Some such texts are given below. They are taken from English tourist guides.

English patterns: (suggested English translations of 'zabytek / zabytki')

Buildings

Brussels, whose history is written in the **buildings** around the famous Grande Place.
Smolensk, a historic city whose **old buildings** are still standing.
Luxemburg's **picturesque buildings** are a delight to visitors.
Stroll about the old city with its numerous bridges and **ancient buildings** (Luxembourg).
Prague has **beautiful buildings** in the baroque style.
Old black and white timbered buildings remain from Elizabethan times.
Worcester, rich in **old buildings**.
Luxembourg, full of **interesting buildings**.
Mediaeval Siena and its **superb buildings**.
After Olomouc and its **historic buildings** come the slopes of the Beskids.
There are more than 200,000 **listed buildings** (sklasyfikowane) in Britain, ranging all the way from public lavatories to stately homes.

Old houses

Winchester, England's ancient capital with its 11th century cathedral and **old houses**.

The word ***architecture*** + adjective

The **1860 architecture** has been preserved and protected as being of historical interest.
Besançon, a fine provincial town with 18th century **architecture**.
Pisa and its **astonishing architecture**.
Munich, city of **superb baroque architecture**.
Amsterdam, a city of **inimitable Dutch architecture**.

Architectural gems (very grand)

The route continues to Pisa, where the leaning tower is only one of the **architectural gems**.

Glories (very grand)

Morning sightseeing (in Florence) will introduce you to its main **glories**.

Treasures (wider connotation – not only buildings)

On the journey to Moscow and Petersburg, where the rich **treasures** of a long history are stored, ...

Wonders (wider connotations – immovables)

We can spend hours enthralled at the **wonders** of the Vatican City and magnificent St. Peter's.

Monuments

Usually confined to ruins, etc.:

Travelling on to Stonehenge, where there is time to inspect the awesome Bronze Age **monuments**, ...

But we also find:

Morning sightseeing in Buda, the old part of the city (Budapest), visiting some of the **historical monuments**.
Stone circles would surely rank as among the most attractive of all our **ancient monuments**.
One author is mainly concerned with **field monuments**.

The words **monuments** and **relics** are often used when 'zabytki' has a general meaning, as in the following texts:

'It is the author's particular strength that he is as much at home among the Byzantine and Norman **relics** as in the treasure house of the classical age, and that his profound feeling for the countryside and its people allows him to fit the **monuments** firmly into their historical and natural perspective.' (*The Companion Guide to Southern Greece*, Brian de Jongh, Collins, St. James's Place, London, 1972, ISBN 0 00 2111241.

This book is meant to help the traveller to identify the surviving **monuments** of the Mycenaean, Archaic and Hellenistic ages.'

Of the **monuments** of the Ottoman period little is left.

In another text, we find:

Milton's cottage, which is 400 years old this year, contains some of his books and pamphlets, a lock of his hair, portraits, and letters, as well as other 17th-century **relics** and furniture. (Note: **relics** here means things which have survived and once belonged to Milton.)

In still another book we find:

They ply the river between Luxor and Aswan. Some of the vessels have the romantic look of museum pieces, Edwardian **relics** from the age of steam. (Note: survivals of the age of steam.)

Remains (rare) – referring only to very distant times, and meaning 'pozostałości', 'ruins', etc.

On through Evora, and its Roman **remains**, ...

Heritage

The more than 200,000 listed buildings in Britain are a massively impressive **architectural heritage**.
who is forced to foot the bill for maintaining the **nation's heritage**.
As a nation, we may be proud of our **cultural heritage**.
Vienna's **architectural heritage** – all monuments – were one and the same to Madame Rubinstein.

Masterpieces

Venice is so full of **masterpieces** that it is impossible to see them all in one day.

Translation:

I. If it is reasonable to assume that 'zabytki' in a given text means *immovables*, we can translate it as: **interesting old buildings, old houses, buildings of historical / historical and architectural interest, buildings of unique historical and architectural interest, fine / magnificent / superb / old architecture, architectural treasures / gems, historical monuments, listed buildings** (if classified as being worthy of preservation).

Thus, if we mean buildings alone, we could translate the following sentences as follows:

Zabytki Krakowa należy natychmiast ratować.
– Something should be done at once to rescue Cracow's **ancient / old / historical buildings** (or **architectural treasures**, or **buildings of historical and architectural interest**, or **beautiful old architecture**).

W Warszawie znajduje się wiele historycznych zabytków, np. kościołów i kamienic.
– Warsaw has many **interesting old buildings**, such as churches and old houses.

Katalog zabytków przeznaczonych na sprzedaż wydano w Wałbrzychu. Wśród takich zabytków znajduje się m.in. zespół pałacowy w Gorzanowie, wybudowany w 1635 r., zajazd w Głuszycy, XVII-wieczny dwór w Jakielnie, a także liczne wiatraki, młyny, karczmy.
– A catalogue of **listed buildings** being offered for sale has been published in Wałbrzych. These include the palace of Gorzanów, built in 1635, an inn at Głuszyca, a seventeenth-century manor at Jakielno, and many windmills, water-mills, and inns.

II. If 'zabytki' refers to *movables* (paintings, religious paraphernalia, *objets d'art*), we can say: **ancient works of art, art treasures, old masterpieces**.

W niektórych kościołach polskich można znaleźć zabytki liczące ponad 700 lat.
– Some Polish churches contain **works of art / art treasures** dating back more than 700 years.

III. If 'zabytki' means both movables and immovables (buildings, fountains, statues, plaques, old cobbled streets, as well as *objets d'art*), we can say: **art and architecture, old buildings and art treasures, glories** (very grand), **treasures, wonders, monuments** (see separate note):

Zabytki Krakowa ulegają powolnemu procesowi zniszczenia.
– The **glories** (the **old buildings and art treasures**) of Cracow are slowly being destroyed.

Note on **monuments** and **relics** as translations of 'zabytki'. The following translations are quite correct:

ochrona zabytków
– the preservation of **ancient monuments**

Nowa Huta stanowi poważne zagrożenie dla zabytków Krakowa.
– The Nowa Huta Steelworks are a serious threat to Cracow's **ancient monuments**.

Note:

a) Do not confuse **relic** with **relict** (see a dictionary).

b) **Relic** and **monument** tend to be used more often with references to the very distant past, such as Antiquity.

c) There is a slight difference between **relic** and **monument**. Possibly **relic** is closer to the meaning *something which has survived*, and refers to something not specially created for commemorative purposes; whereas **monument**, while also meaning *a survival*, has another meaning as well, that of *adding to the glory* of a past age, etc.

d) **Monument** (often singular) can mean either a statue, memorial, etc. (especially commemorative), or, particularly in the plural, it may mean something of a more general nature not specially created for a commemorative purpose, but which nevertheless reminds us of the nature and grandeur of a past period. These observations may be applied to translation:

> Kolumny, które tutaj widzimy, są zabytkami kultury doryckiej.
> – The columns which we see here are relics of the Doric culture.
> Pałac w Rybokartach z przełomu XVIII i XIX wieku należy do najwspanialszych zabytków naszej kultury.
> – The palace at Rybokarty, dating from the 18th and 19th centuries, is one of the most splendid **monuments** of our culture.

e) Nevertheless, when translating the Polish 'zabytki', it is wiser to avoid the English word **monuments**. Used in the singular, the English word **monument** almost always means 'pomnik'. If we use **monuments** (meaning not 'pomniki' but 'zabytki') in the plural at all, it is safer to use a qualifying phrase or adjective, e.g. **monuments of a past age, monuments of the Minoan culture, ancient monuments, historical monuments. Monuments** in English has a low frequency – very much less than that of the Polish 'zabytki'.

f) Do not say **architectural monuments**.

g) Translate 'historyczny zabytek' as **ancient monument**.

i) **Relics** is also a word that should be used with great caution.

In translating the phrase 'zwiedzać zabytki tego miasta', it would be wrong to say 'visit the **relics** of that city'. It would be right, however, to say '**relics** of a civilisation, **relics** of a culture, **relics** of a period, etc'. We should translate 'zwiedzać zabytki naszego miasta' as:

– make a tour of the **old parts of the city**, or:
– tour the **places of historical interest** in the city.

IV. If 'zabytki' means the treasures (*movable* and *immovable*) belonging to the whole nation, we can say **national heritage**, or sometimes **cultural heritage**.

Naszym obowiązkiem jest chronić zabytki w naszym kraju.
– It is our duty to preserve the **national heritage**.

V. If we have 'zabytek' meaning an outstanding building such as a church, we can sometimes say: **gem of architecture, architectural gem, architectural jewel**.

Ten wyjątkowy kościół jest zabytkiem sztuki.
– This unique church is a **gem of architecture**.

Note that in this sentence we would translate 'sztuka' by **architecture** (not **art**). It would be wrong, or, rather, inadequate, to translate 'zabytkiem sztuki' as a **work of art**. It would also be wrong to translate it as **an arts relic**, or **relic of art**.

VI. 'Zabytek klasy 0' – We do not know as yet how to translate this into English. Until the proper equivalent is found (if it does exist), we could say 'a **top-grade** building of historical and architectural interest', or perhaps 'an architecture **gem**', or 'a **Grade A** building'.

Warnings:

1. Never translate 'zabytki' by **remnants** (see a dictionary).
2. The English adjective **monumental** does not mean 'zabytkowy', but 'huge and imposing'.
3. Do not use the adjective **antique** with buildings, etc. It can be used only with movable objects such as maps, furniture, china, glass.
4. **Ancient** generally means: belonging to a remoter past than old. Mills, taverns, etc. are old, not ancient.
5. Avoid over-use of the word **historical**, because the range of its applications is much narrower in English than in Polish. In Polish one could apply the adjective 'zabytkowy' to an old mill, bridge, inn, etc. But in English one would use the adjective **old** not **historical**, because these objects are not important enough to be called **historical**. We say an **old** mill, an **old** inn, etc.

It is ***WRONG*** to say 'historical masterpiece'. One should say: **old masterpiece**.

6. It is ***WRONG*** to say: This column represents the **heritage** of the Dorian culture'. A heritage belongs to a people, to a nation. One may easily fall into the trap of confusing **heritage** meaning 'spuścizna'(abstract values), with **heritage** meaning 'zabytki' (concrete objects). When translating 'zabytki', it is safer to confine oneself to the term **national heritage**, meaning ancient monuments, art objects, etc.

Spis omówionych haseł

Wydawnictwo Naukowe PWN SA
Wydanie II – 4 dodruk
Arkuszy drukarskich 10,5
Skład i łamanie: FOTOTYPE
Druk ukończono we wrześniu 2008 r.
Druk i oprawa: GRAFMAR Sp. z o.o.
36-100 Kolbuszowa Dolna, ul. Wiejska 43